I0475834

"Most people have accepted mediocrity - in all areas of life. Don't be one of them. The game has changed. It is now possible to get your money right, create your ideal lifestyle, and live life fully on your terms at a young age. Daniel not only realizes this, he maximizes this massive opportunity and he wants to help you do the same."
- Peter Voogd (peterjvoogd.com), #1 Bestselling author of 6 Months to 6 Figures and Founder of Game Changers Movement (gamechangersmovement.com)

"We're living in an age where wealth is a choice. It is now possible to create wealth, take control, and live your definition of success, even at a young age. Daniel is taking advantage of this and you can do the same by using his proven wealth-creation strategies."
- Austin Netzley, #1 Best-selling author of Make Money, Live Wealthy and Founder of Epic Launch, the leading book marketing team

Join the Community!

Be a part of the Cure Mediocrity community on Facebook.
We will fill it up with tons of ambitious, world-class people.
Facebook.com/groups/cure-mediocrity

#CureMediocrity

THE
CURE FOR
MEDIOCRITY

CREATE WEALTH, ACHIEVE FREEDOM,
AND LIVE THE WORLD-CLASS LIFESTYLE

DANIEL HAUGE

The Cure for Mediocrity

Copyright © 2017 Daniel Hauge
All rights reserved.

No part of this book may be reproduced in any form or by any electronic or mechanical means, including information storage and retrieval systems, without permission in writing from the author. The only exception is by a reviewer, who may quote short excerpts in a published review.

Cover design by Paul Mavis
Copy editing by Jacqueline Rapetti
Proofreading by Oliver Jackson

Written by,
Daniel Hauge (www.danielhauge.com)

1st edition.
Printed in the USA.

ISBN-13: 978-1544043296

The information presented herein represents the view of the author as of the date of publication. This book is presented for informational purposes only. Due to the rate at which conditions change, the author reserves the right to alter and update his opinions based on new conditions. While every attempt has been made to verify the information in this book, neither the author nor his affiliates/partners assume any responsibility for errors, inaccuracies, or omissions

To my mom and my brother:
You're the most supportive family I could've ever wished for.
Thank you.

To my father, who passed away when I was 11 years old:
You taught me to fight and never give up when things get tough.
And no matter how tough life gets, always care and be there for others.
Thank You.

To Emil, Auguste, and Marko:
You're amazing people and great friends.
I would not have been where I am today without you.
Thank you.

To everyone else who's supporting me:
Your support means more to me than you think.
Thank you.

To all the 'haters' in my life, telling me I won't make it:
You motivate me to prove you wrong.
I'm gonna make you look stupid.

Contents

INTRODUCTION

Out of 100 people who start working at age 25, only five will, according to Statistic Brain Research Institute, be financially independent at age 65. The rest? They'll either be working, dead or depending on friends, relatives, and Social Security to get by.

Spend the first 25 years of your life going to school. Your education and studies will be prioritized over nearly everything else. Next, you'll get an "acceptable" job with minimal freedom and a limited income. You'll save everything you don't need to survive and put it into savings.

Do this for 40 years.

One day, at age 65, you will be able to beautifully retire and live an amazing life (if you're in the lucky 5%, of course. To be honest, though, you're probably still gonna be working, or at least depending on your family to survive... but don't tell anyone that.) Oh, and by the way, if you put a little bit more air in your tires you can save on gas. This will shorten the journey from 40 years to 39 years, 11 months and 2 weeks.

Does this not sounds like a wonderful recipe for an amazing life filled with experiences, freedom, happiness, prosperity, fulfillment and overall satisfaction?

Now, what I'm about to do is *very dangerous*. I'm going to do something that I've been called a lot of negative things for doing. I've been called confused, stupid, greedy, misinformed, ignorant and I'm pretty sure at one point I've been called retarded. I'm gonna do it anyway, though.

I'm going to state my honest opinion: I do not find this way of living very appealing. There, I said it.

The problem with this way of doing things is that it's setting us up for mediocrity in all areas of our lives. When we're trapped in a job, it can be challenging to find the freedom, and the finances, to travel whenever we want to. It can be difficult to have time and energy to take care of ourselves - mentally and physically. Overall, it becomes very challenging to live life to the fullest and really reach our potential financially, physically, emotionally, etc. This is very unfortunate because we ALL have the opportunity to do more, give more and be more.

LET'S BE HONEST

First of all, in this book, I'm gonna tell you what you *need* to hear and not what you *want* to hear. There's a lot of money in telling you that what your parents told you is the right way to do it. However, someone has to tell people the truth. And, since no one else is gonna tell you these things, I will. Your days of being misinformed and brainwashed are over! Well, maybe not. Everyone, including your friends and family, will still tell you all kinds of BS. They don't do this to be evil. They feed you this BS because they just don't know any better.

This book should, hopefully, shift your mindset about wealth and freedom, perhaps giving you a new perspective.

Every piece of information in this book has been used by some of the most successful and wealthy people on the planet. There's a huge amount of successful people out there who we can learn a ton from. So, I decided to go on a studying spree. The last couple of years I've spent all my time, energy and money on studying successful people and then testing what I'd learned.

Within this book, you will only find the most powerful, valuable and extremely useful information. Everything has been used to create extraordinary results by myself, or others.

You know all these young millionaires around the world just living the dream? How cool would it be to have them teach you how they did it? How powerful would it be to pick their brains? You don't need to because I already did. Just read this book.

After reading this book, you will have the resources, techniques, and the guidance to create real wealth and achieve freedom. This will make it possible for you to reach your potential in all other areas of life. You will no longer be a slave to society, the system or your own limiting beliefs. Instead, you will be able to live life on *your* terms and *only* your terms.

You will know how to achieve extreme freedom which will provide you the opportunity to travel and see the world, stay in shape, do what you want to when you want to and, ultimately, live life like you've always wanted.

I'm proud to say that I've already helped a lot of people shift their perspectives on money, freedom, and the extraordinary lifestyle. Many of them started off with a very skeptical outlook on my ideas. However, I tend to talk a lot when the conversation is about living life to the fullest and getting rich. Eventually, people started to actually listen to what I had to say. Some of them even took action and implemented my ideas. Those are the ones who now say I've changed their lives.

If you read this book, put it on the bookshelf and then forget everything about it, here's what will happen: You will get a fresh new perspective on life and money and you'll know how to take your life to the level you've always dreamed of. Not much in your life will change, though.

If you read this book, take massive action and you implement the strategies I'll be talking about, here's what will happen: You'll start seeing massive results or, at least, have complete clarity on how to get them. You will be on your way toward your ideal scene and your vision (more on this later).

I suggest you read this book, take massive action and chase your vision and desires. Don't wait for someone else to come into your life with a pink wand to magically make the changes for you. The only way to change your life is to *change your life*. Only you can decide if you get to live the amazing, next-level lifestyle or not. **The time is now. Take action.**

HOW THIS BOOK IS ORGANIZED

Part 1. In the first part, I'll talk about the system and our society. Also, I'll be talking about mediocrity in general.

Part 2. This is where I'll reveal what *The Cure for Mediocrity* really is. This part is the most important when it comes to freedom and the world-class lifestyle. In this part, I'll reveal why some people work for 20 to 40 years without getting wealthy, while others get rich within a few years.

Part 3. This part is all about the money. I'll be talking about real, no-bullshit wealth creation techniques, strategies, and principles used by the world's wealthiest people. Spoiler alert: It's not to drink less Starbucks coffee to save a few bucks every month.

Part 4. In this part, I'll be talking about how you can become a person capable of achieving massive success - financially, emotionally, mentally, and physically.

P.S. There will be a bulleted chapter summary after each chapter. Those are crucial to read. Don't skip them.

WARNING!

This book is extremely controversial in many ways. I understand that a lot of people will take some of the advice in this book as an attack against them. I want everyone to realize that many of my friends and family members are living very differently than I am. They're still the most amazing people on the planet.

I appreciate the fact that we can all have different opinions on specific topics. This is what makes the world interesting. Again, to anyone who might feel offended while reading this book, I want you to know that I do not think less about you because of your opinions.

I would really appreciate if you read this book with an open mind and a desire to see things from a different perspective. This is not meant to be some kind of battle. It's meant to give you some fresh, innovative ideas on how to do things. Perhaps we can start a positive debate with this book.

If you're ready to go into this book with an open mind, ready to see the world from a different angle, and you take massive action on what I'll be talking about, I think you will find this book very powerful and valuable.

P.S. If you find anything in the book that offends you, is misleading, or needs an edit, please let me know at Daniel@Cure-Mediocrity.com.

ENJOY!

PART 1:

THE MEDIOCRE

SYSTEM

"The greatest form of control is where you think you're free, when you're being fundamentally manipulated and dictated to. One form of dictatorship is being in a prison cell and you can see the bars and touch it. The other one is sitting in a prison cell but you can't see the bars so you think you're free." – David Icke

I'm not suggesting that we're living in a dictatorship. However, that quote from David Icke, English writer and public speaker, has a lot of truth to it. We compare ourselves to those who live in other places around the planet and we think we have the most amazing freedom. We believe we're free and we can do whatever we want.

The system is doing everything it can to have us live the most wonderful life filled with freedom and opportunities, right? *Wrong.* Nothing could be further from the truth.

[1]

SET UP FOR MEDIOCRITY

We're being suppressed. Set up for mediocrity. Brainwashed. We're being force-fed *limiting beliefs.* Having a limiting belief means that what you believe, and how you perceive a specific situation, can hold you back and limit your capabilities and opportunities.

Limiting beliefs are extremely dangerous because they steal all hopes of reaching our actual potential. They're also contagious. This means that, when living in a society where everyone has limiting beliefs, it can be very difficult and almost inevitable not to have them ourselves.

Try it right now. Tell your friends and family that you want to be very wealthy in two or three years. They'll either tell you you're being immature and naive or they will smile and tell you that it's good to be optimistic, while laughing a bit because what you're suggesting seems ridiculous. Not many people believe that there are other opportunities than to go to school, get a degree and then work for 40 years. Because of these limiting beliefs, we're walking around feeling like this is all there is when it's really not. We're being set up for mediocrity.

IT'S EASY TO CONTROL SOMEONE IN A CAGE

So, why are we being set up for mediocrity by the system? *Why can't we just all do what we love to do?* Why do we have to go through the mediocre system (school, degree, job, etc.) just to do something we don't like? Because that's a lot easier to handle than someone taking risks and doing his or her own thing.

Let me tell you what happened when I, as a 16-year-old, decided to quit school to follow my entrepreneurial visions. I immediately had education advisers, people who specialized in getting young people educated, all over my ass. They would call me several times a week to convince me to go back to school, take up an apprenticeship or get some other kind of education. They were freaking out about the fact that I was going to do something different from the traditional way, even though I told them exactly what I planned to do.

I told the world that I wanted to become an entrepreneur and follow my dreams. Immediately everyone wanted me to quit and go back to school, trying to convince me not to do something great. If that's not suppression, I don't know what is.

Now, I realize that not everyone can be living the dream. A society can't function properly with everyone being pop stars, athletes and ninjas (yes, that was my dream when I was little... imagine how cool that could be). We need people who take the 'normal' jobs and I really appreciate everyone contributing to society like that. Here's the thing: there are enough people like that and there always will be. Trust me, there is never going to be a shortage of people living normal, traditional lives. Since there are so many people who go the traditional route, you have the opportunity to do so much more than what's *normal.*

There will always be people who want comfort, security, and safety. For this reason, there will always be tremendous opportunity for risk-takers. It would be a terrible shame if we, as aspiring achievers and dream chasers, wasted our potential. My motto in life is: *Don't Waste Your Potential.*

GET RICH, SLOW

One of the limiting beliefs we're being sold on is the get-rich-slow game plan. The idea that the way to prosperity and wealth is through working hard our entire lives while saving a little piece of our salaries each month. And then, we hope that everything goes well. We hope we can get a decent job. We hope we can keep the job we have. We hope the stock market runs smoothly. We hope our homes increase in value. We hope we get to retire before our bodies get too tired to enjoy it. I'm here to tell you something you must understand if you're looking for the amazing lifestyle. A game plan built on hope, luck and tailwind is NOT ideal.

Any game plan suggesting that you have to wait until you're 65 years old to win is extremely ridiculous in my opinion. *Why wait?* Why live our entire lives just preparing for an amazing lifestyle when we're 65? I really don't understand how that appeals to anyone!

Also, I want you to realize that, when following the traditional way of doing things, a nice retirement at age 65 is the BEST-case scenario. Only 5% of 65-year-olds are financially independent. This means that the nice retirement at 65, which I'm finding everything but appealing, is actually what only the top 5% gets. What does the rest get for working 40 years in a row while saving what's left? They get to keep working, die or rely on friends, family and Social Security. Would I like to sign up for that? *Absolutely fucking not.*

Only 4% of workers believe they'll be able to stop working before the age of 55. So, with the get-rich-slow gameplan, your chances of retiring before you have grey hair and a knee surgery are almost non-existent. Don't limit yourself like that!

Let's look at this fact list to see how much get-rich-slow should turn you off (these statistics are from the US):

- 4% of workers believe they can retire before age 55.

- 5% of 65 year olds are financially independent.

- 80% of 30-54 year olds believe they won't have enough money for retirement.

- At age 65, the average person has a retirement savings 1/10 of what financial experts recommend for independence.

- As of 2013, 90% of seniors age 65 or older were receiving help from Social Security.

- 63% of seniors 65 or older are dependent on Social Security, relatives, friends or charity.

As you can see, this amazing way of doing things is really not that amazing at all. Yet we all work extremely hard to achieve this lifestyle.

If your road to wealth is through a long, traditional education, a decent job and saving money, you will not experience true prosperity. Trust me. However, this is what everyone wants us to believe. Most people believe it and the reason they're doing that is because they haven't been properly introduced to other opportunities. I want you to realize, though, that there are tons of other more efficient routes toward wealth.

You will, hopefully, know a lot more about these routes after reading this book. For now, just know that the get-rich-slow game plan everyone is trying to sell you on will not get you wealthy. Especially not while you're still young and able to enjoy your money.

EDUCATION

Now, I'm pretty sure a group of conservative, 55-year-old teachers and professors will try to find me and come whoop my ass. I'm willing to take that chance, though, because someone has to speak the truth about these things.

We've been raised to believe that school and traditional education is the most amazing thing. School is what prepares us for the real world and sets us up for a world full of opportunities with which we know exactly what to do because we've learned about it in school.

This is what we've been influenced, by society, our family, our friends and everyone else, to believe and think about the school system. School is just the greatest thing and without it we would never know anything about anything.

This is not the reality.

The reality is that we're learning the wrong things! **We're not being set up for a life full of opportunities because what we learn in school has nothing to do with the real world.** The things we absolutely need to learn, we don't. And the things we have no use for, ever, we get force-fed with. This is why so many people, when finished with school, have no idea what to do with their lives. We suddenly realize that we're not in a classroom anymore.

Maybe instead of the Pythagorean theorem, we could be taught the psychology of making others happy? The things we learn in school need to be much more useful in the real world than what they are now.

Here's a list of things kids are currently learning about in school:

- Plant cells and other eukaryotic cells and their organelles.
- Geometry and polygons.
- Memorizing dates in history.
- Hand-writing in cursive.
- The periodic table of elements.
- Poetry.

Now, I realize that a future biologist needs to know about cells, a poet needs to know poetry and a chemist would have to know the periodic table of elements. But are these not things that could be learned in an optional class? What about the 99.5% of people who do not need it? Why does everyone need to learn these things just because one or two in every class might use it *a little bit*? This feels like a huge waste of time, money, energy and resources in general.

Here's a list of things kids *should* be learning in school:

- Personal finance - investing, taxes, etc.
- The psychology of happiness, fulfillment, etc.
- Love, people, emotional intelligence, relationships, etc.

- How to get the most out of life, traveling, experiences, memories, adventures, etc.

- Health, nutrition, fitness, etc.

- Entrepreneurship, starting projects, creating, etc.

- Confidence, self-esteem, courage, etc.

- How to handle fear, anxiety, depression, adversity, etc.

Now, I'm not saying that this idea can change the world. *But it can.* Imagine what your country or the world would look like if we were taught these skills in school. Imagine the world we would be living in if everyone had at least basic knowledge on these topics. Please realize how amazing this world would be. Yet how much do we learn about these things? How many classes did you have on confidence or emotional intelligence? How many did you have on geometry or poetry?

Something's not right.

Polygons and the psychology of happiness are both very useful. The difference is that polygons are useful to the 0.5% of people who will use them. The psychology of happiness is useful to 100% of the world.

Why don't we start school with teaching children the things that everyone could benefit from? Why don't we teach them how to be happy, how to have confidence in themselves and even how money works? What would the world look like if every person learned all these things at a young age? Some 65 year olds still have no knowledge about these topics. In my opinion, the school system should focus on teaching things that everyone can benefit from.

Now, we obviously still need to learn how to write and how to calculate simple math. Save the mitochondria for an optional class to the children interested in biology.

Another thing I don't like about the school system is that we get taught *what* to think and not *how* to think. **We get educated instead of being taught how to educate ourselves.** Instead of being told the answers, why don't we learn how to ask questions? Why do I have to memorize who the 17th president was? I can Google that. Why should I memorize how a plant cell is organized? I can Google that.

We're living in an age where it is no longer beneficial to remember a lot of random facts. It's beneficial to be able to ask the right questions.

Einstein was once asked how many feet are in a mile, to which he replied, "I don't know. Why should I fill my brain with facts I can find in two minutes in any standard reference book?" This was over 50 years ago when we didn't have the technology we do today. His point was strong back then and it is 200 times stronger today. Einstein wasn't interested in wasting brain power on remembering random facts. He would rather use his brain to come up with new theories and to ask questions.

The problem with the school system is that it refuses to continuously evolve and adapt.

Think about where we were with technology 10 or 15 years ago. Now, think about where we were with the school system 100 or 150 years ago. When I think about this, my facial posture is a nice mix of an ugly cringe and a childish little smile. Our entire world has been completely revolutionized technologically in the last 15 years. The school system? I mean, the teachers don't hit children anymore and we now have better blackboards. Apart from that, we haven't really accomplished much in the last 100 years.

What happens when everything but the school system adapts and evolves? Everyone dies in a hellish rain of fire. Well, bad things happen at least.

What will happen is that the school system's teaching will become irrelevant, which it already has. Unless we start evolving and improving the school system soon, we end up with a completely irrelevant and useless system. I seriously cannot believe that we keep teaching the same things our grandparents were taught. This does not make sense because we're living in a completely different world than the one our grandparents grew up in.

So, do I hate school and everything it stands for? Absolutely not. Education is crucial and it's important that we teach children how the world works. We have to teach children and we have to make it mandatory because everyone needs it. I just really disagree with the choice of material being taught. If school taught more relevant topics, I would be a huge supporter and I would probably still be in school.

Should you stay in school or should you drop out? Well, this is my opinion:

Stay in school if...

- You don't know what you want to do.

- You know what you want to do and you believe school can teach you useful and relevant material regarding your topic faster and more effectively than you could by yourself.

- Your dream job requires it.

- You like/need the social aspect of going to school.

- It feels right for you.

- Your parents know where I live.

Don't go to school if...

- You hate school and it's not a requirement for future jobs you're interested in.

- You know what you want to do and you know you can teach yourself the right material faster and more effectively than a teacher in a classroom. (You often can.)

- You want to be an entrepreneur.

- You put yourself in debt.

- It doesn't feel right for you.

You need to do what feels right for you. Again, I'm just here with viable suggestions that I know work. I challenge you to get out of your comfort zone and try looking at things with a new perspective.

Always remember, though, that no matter what you choose to do regarding school, you should ALWAYS educate yourself on personal development, health, wealth, happiness, confidence and other really important areas in your life. Always grow and learn. You should never let school interfere with your education.

CHAPTER BULLET POINTS:

- We're being oppressed and brainwashed to settle for mediocrity.

- Limiting beliefs are beliefs that prevent us from reaching our potential. These beliefs are highly contagious.

- There will always be massive opportunity for risk takers who chase their visions.

- Get-rich-slow, the game plan based on working 40 years at a job, contributing to one's 401(k) and buying a nice home, used to make people wealthy. It doesn't anymore.

- Get-rich-slow is based on hope, luck, and tailwind.

- The world is changing, but society and the system are not.

[2]

2%

I'm going to start this chapter by throwing a long ass quote in your face. It's a quote from Joe Rogan from *The Joe Rogan Experience*. Enjoy.

> *"So society gets wrapped around becoming a part of a machine. Society, instead of becoming a bunch of individuals that are expressing themselves in unique ways, and everybody sort-of borrows and shares and sells this and you sell that and we all sort of figure out how we can contribute in a society, we got sidetracked and diverted into these boxes that they call companies and corporations. And we got stuck into these containers, they call cubicles or offices, and we got forced into this system.*
>
> *And this is your life now: no natural behavior, everybody's wearing clothes they don't wanna wear, everybody's showing up doing something they don't want to do, they have no connection to. That's the problem with our society.*
>
> *And then what's the reward for all this stuff? Go home and get a big TV. You go home and you get a shiny belt buckle. You're gonna get a nice purse. You're gonna get shoes that you couldn't afford last week. And every week we're chasing*

down this new object, and every week we're trying to fill this hole, this sad shadow of a life that we've been left with after work."

God, this quote is so negative and pessimistic. Sadly, though, it's extremely true. I'm glad some people have the balls to say stuff like that. *This truth needs to be told.*

We're told to be "realistic" which, by the way, is the most useless word in the English language. At first, we don't want to be realistic. We all had huge dreams as children. However, after getting the *be realistic* rejection every single day from society, we start to doubt if it's even possible. Eventually, we give up on our dreams and we go for something that doesn't require anything. Yay, we finally found something *realistic* that makes us live up to 2% of our potential. Woo hoo.

"Being realistic is the most commonly traveled road to mediocrity." - Will Smith

I'm here to tell you that, if you go to school, get an education, get a job you don't like and you clock in and clock out your entire life because nothing else is *realistic,* you need to stop right now.

If you're wondering why this chapter is called "2%" it's because that's how much of their potential mediocre people are reaching.

Since all of our big dreams have been suppressed or eliminated, we accept that we have to go to school and then settle for a job. Because of our limited salary and our 1 or 2 vacations a year, we do not have a ton of freedom. We don't even have the time/energy to care for our health - physically or mentally. We get stressed out and we have no energy because of our lack of healthy habits - which makes everything else even harder.

With all of these important areas of our life at a low, it's hard to stay motivated and excited about life, which makes everything even harder. As a result, we end up reaching 2% of our overall potential.

Wasting your potential in life is like finding $4 million and then grabbing $13. It's a damn shame because you had the opportunity to get, be and give so much more.

Please realize that everyone who listens to society and settles, instead of chasing their dreams, is reaching 2% of their potential in life.

THE RESULT?

As you can probably imagine, a society full of people reaching 2% of their potential is not a very good thing. It's actually quite dangerous because when an entire society is living up to just 2% of its potential, it's hard to do anything to change it and two very dangerous things can happen:

Result 1. Our entire world will live up to 2% of its potential. If everyone living in a society lives up to 2% of their potential, how can our society reach its maximum potential? It can't. It will only be a fraction of how great it could be.

Result 2. You will struggle reaching your own potential. When everyone around you, including your loved ones and friends, are doing absolutely nothing with their lives, it will influence you. Now, I'm not saying that if your Uncle John is at a mediocre job, you will have a miserable life. What I am saying, though, is that if everyone you surround yourself with is doing things one way, your chances of doing things that same way are dramatically higher.

You see, the people you spend the most time with is one of the biggest determinators of your future success or failure. Jim Rohn, a personal development legend, said that we are the average of the five people we spend the most time with. If we adopt the beliefs, opinions, limitations, values, etc. from the people around us, can you see how dangerous it is to live in a mediocre society full of limiting beliefs? This is what's happening. The majority is mediocre with a ton of limiting beliefs. Since we get influenced by what the majority does, we, too, start to think that way. We then become a part of the mediocre majority ourselves.

"You show me your friends. I'll show you your future." - Marc Mero

When I started having dreams about doing something big and different, I would tell everyone about it. I would talk about it with all my friends, with my family and sometimes even with strangers. I would go on about how I was going to change the world by becoming an entrepreneur. I was extremely passionate about my ambitions.

What I quickly realized, though, is that mediocre people do not understand ambitious dreams. A lot of my friends would laugh and some of my family would pity me and feel sorry for me because *I was setting myself up for failure* by not getting a degree. Imagine that. People you respect and look up to are telling you to not follow your dreams - sometimes even while laughing at you. *That* is discouraging.

Why did they not understand my ambitious dreams? Because my dreams were from a whole other world than the one they were living in. They had been influenced and pulled down to mediocrity by society and now they were a part of that society themselves. They simply could not understand that there was more to life than the traditional school, education and job lifestyle. Never had they ever known anyone who had done it. And every time they had seen someone do big things, someone else would tell them that the only way to do that is through luck or rich parents. So, I don't really blame them for laughing and not understanding me.

When talking to mediocre people, you have to realize that suggesting huge, ambitious dreams is like talking about super heroes, demons and pink unicorns. They don't understand it because they haven't ever been given any kind of proof that it's possible. When they do get proof, they refuse to accept it as evidence and they stay in their little boxes.

> *"You can't discuss the ocean with a well frog - he's limited by the space he lives in. You can't discuss ice with a summer insect - he's bound to a single season." - <u>Zhuang Zhou</u>*

This is why it is absolutely crucial to spend your time with like-minded people and with people who challenge you to think big. You need to spend time around people who have higher standards about life. Do this, and you will see your life change almost immediately.

I realized that for me to not lose my ambition, passion and desire for the next level, I had to be around like-minded people. "Oh, that's great Daniel, I'm just going to start hanging out with millionaires, athletes and game-changers then. Thanks."

It can indeed be very difficult to find like-minded people and randomly connect. At least, *it was*. Not long ago, if you wanted to be in some kind of group or community, you would have to go meet people in person. This is not the case anymore.

There are tons of communities like this on the internet that you can join. Interested in sports? Join a sport community or group. Interested in entrepreneurship? Join one of the many entrepreneurship communities out there.

I found an amazing membership program filled with like-minded people. There was a lot of courses and information on the site, but the main reason I joined was that I would be surrounded by people with higher standards and bigger dreams. This was a complete game-changer. It was like heaven had opened up for me. Everyone I spoke to was as excited and ambitious about life as I was. Suddenly, I went from everyone around me bringing me down to everyone lifting me up and bringing me closer to the amazing lifestyle.

Trust me, being extremely intentional about who you spend time with will be a huge game-changer in your life. It will without a doubt change your life like you never thought was possible.

In the future, I'll definitely be creating a membership platform myself. It's so incredibly powerful.

EVERYTHING MAINSTREAM SUCKS

Is everyone you know living the dream? Is everyone you know traveling the world like you want to? Does everyone you know have financial freedom and tons of free time? Are all your friends and family members completely fulfilled?

If not, then why would you follow what everybody's doing? **Why follow a road you know won't lead you to where you want to be?**

We look around and we see misery. We see society, including friends and family, walking around in a mediocre, unfulfilling life. They're tired of their jobs but can't quit because they're slaves - a part of a machine. They're tired of their health and their bodies but can't change it because they lack energy and time. They love to travel, experience and enjoy free time, yet they rarely have the opportunities to do so.

We promise ourselves that we won't live like that. We will not create a lifestyle like that for ourselves. We want more than that.

Yet what do we do? We go to these people for advice. We ask these people how to live life and we take their word. I've seen depressed people, extremely unfulfilled in every area of life, give their children the exact same advice that got them to this depressing lifestyle. And even though we see how that worked out for those people, we still listen and we follow their advice because they're older and more experienced. We then end up exactly like the ones we didn't want to end up like. Our dreams and ambitions slowly die.

We know exactly what we want and what we don't. There are two paths. There is the path toward our dreams and there is a path toward the opposite. 95% of people decide to take the second path. We know we don't want to end up unfulfilled and unhappy, yet we follow the exact road that will take us there. We know we want to travel the world and have endless freedom. We want to be limitless. Yet we still educate ourselves (or at least go to school) for a specific job that sets us up for a life as a slave.

Why do we want one thing but do the opposite? Because it's *safe* and comfortable to do what everyone else is doing. It's scary to do the opposite. It's terrifying to go against everything you've been taught since you were little. *What if it fails?* What if everyone says *I told you so?* What if people will look down on me for not following the system?

> *"They will say that you're on the wrong road, if it's your own."* - Antonio Porchia

It is scary and it will definitely feel unnatural to go against what everyone else is doing. However, there is something you must realize if you hope to live the lifestyle you dream about. **Follow what mediocre people are doing and you, too, will be mediocre.** Everything mainstream sucks. Don't follow what everyone is doing because everyone is not happy and fulfilled. These people are certainly not living the lifestyle you desire.

You will not win by doing what everyone else is doing. Think about all the successful people on this planet. The greatest CEOs didn't follow "the system." Nor did the greatest athletes. **Every successful person became successful because he or she did something that others weren't doing.**

Now, let me ask you: Which one of the following two statements has the highest chance of being said by an NFL player?

1. "So, yeah, I just focused on school and on doing my homework. At age 26, I graduated and got my degree in art history. Then I used that degree to win the Superbowl."

Sounds unlikely... What about this one?

2. "Everyone kept telling me to go to school and get a degree. My entire family and all my friends were doing things that way. I

just knew I wanted to do something different. I went and did my own thing and I practiced and improved until I eventually made it happen."

Successful people are never the ones who followed the mediocre, mainstream society. I'm here to tell you that, if you desire the amazing lifestyle, stop following mediocrity.

If you want to win in life, you have to follow the right people. There is no way around it. Following a proven path is absolutely crucial - as long as it's the *right* path. Follow people with the same values as you.

THE CONVEYOR BELT OF LIFE

You may start to wonder, when this mediocre way of doing things is so terrible, why do so many people, including perfectly intelligent people, decide to travel this road of mediocrity? Simple. Because we live on something I call *the conveyor belt of life.*

A conveyor belt is the rubber belt you often see in factories. It's the piece of rubber that goes around and around while carrying materials from one station to another. It does this repeatedly. Over and over...

Society is living life on a conveyor belt. We're born, we go to school, we get a job, we retire and then we die. We teach our kids to do the same. Our kids will teach their kids to do the same. We keep doing the same things over and over again.

But that's not the worst part. The worst part is that we do the same things over and over again without ever improving, evolving or adapting.

In a factory, if the company decided to change their product line or their way of producing products, they would change the way their conveyor system worked - moving their conveyor belts around and adjusting them to be useful and relevant to their new circumstances.

Unfortunately, we don't do this when it comes to societies and systems. Our entire system was built to be optimal for the way we lived when it was built. Here's the thing we need to realize, though. We live in a whole other world than we did 100, 50, 20 or even 5 years ago. We should, for that reason, not be using the system we used back then. We should adapt to our current circumstances and environments.

We're doing what our parents were taught by their parents who were taught by their parents. This obviously cannot be very effective because we're not living in our grandparent's world anymore. **Our system is not adapting because we're never adjusting our conveyor belts.** We just keep doing what we've always done and we try our best to protect this way of doing things. This is dangerous!

As we learn from plants and animals, everything that doesn't adapt to its surroundings will die. Our society, too, will die, or at least become less and less effective, if we don't start to realize that our world is changing. When we've realized that putting people through a 20-year-long school system and teaching the wrong things, is an old and inefficient way of doing things, we need to accept it. Then we need to adapt.

> *"It is not the strongest of the species that survive, nor the most intelligent, but the one most responsive to change." - Charles Darwin*

"In the struggle for survival, the fittest win out at the expense of their rivals because they succeeded in adapting themselves best to their environment." - Charles Darwin again

Since the system won't adapt, you have to jump off the conveyor belt and start adapting yourself. Later in this book, I will talk a lot more about how to adapt and how to take advantage of the world we currently live in. You'll realize that, if you decide to adapt to this new world, the opportunities and possibilities are endless.

For now, though, really think about whether or not this traditional conveyor belt is for you.

ARE WE VICTIMS?

It's really starting to sound like I'm a bitch. A crybaby. A *victim.* I'm just a miserable person who's here to whine and blame everything and everyone but himself. I can't take responsibility for my own life so I blame the system and our society, right?

This is actually not the case at all.

I've been completely miserable, even suicidal, and I've been extremely fulfilled and happy. I've been broke, on my way to a life of no opportunities, and I've been on the road to complete financial freedom and a life full of opportunities and possibilities. I've been at the bottom, struggling to get out of bed in the morning, and I've been at the emotional top, feeling like I owned the world.

Both scenarios were because of me. And ONLY because of me.

You see, I believe that life is 3% circumstances and 97% perception, perspective and beliefs. What we get from life is determined by what we do, how we react to events and a lot of other things that we can control. Remember, there are always people who have been through worse things than you but are happier than you currently are. There are also always people who have been through nothing compared to you but are currently miserable. Life is what you make it.

Society is offering us a very bad way of doing things. Society is offering us a lifestyle full of stress, misery, lack of freedom and lack of fulfillment.

What you need to realize, though, is that if you decide to grab this opportunity for a traditional life, then it's on you. You might be influenced by family, friends, teachers, etc., but if you made the decision to follow the path to mediocrity, then that's your decision.

But you don't understand, dude, my family is forcing me, you say. Well, having a family that doesn't support you in your decision to do your own thing is very unfortunate. Keep in mind, though, that the reason they're telling you that is because they love you and want the best for you. So, if you really decide to do something else other than the traditional, mediocre way of doing things, I think your parents would be proud that you made a decision like that. Especially if they see that it makes you happy.

Please realize that if you decide to follow society's mediocre road, then you're the only person to blame when you end up with mediocre results. If the mediocre road you followed made you mediocre, don't blame the road, blame the person who decided to follow that road - **you.** Mediocre people didn't become mediocre because of the system's shitty game plan. Mediocre people got mediocre results because they decided to follow and accept a mediocre game plan.

If you want extraordinary results and the world-class lifestyle, don't follow a mediocre game plan.

Imagine this. You're having an amazing day, just enjoying life. You've finished your workout and you just came out of the shower. Now it's time for a delicious and well-earned breakfast. You're in the sun, enjoying your breakfast and everything else this wonderful life has to offer. Suddenly, this gigantic, enormous dog walks up to you and takes a huge, massive crap.

Now, there are really only two things you can choose to do here. You can decide to walk away and do your own thing, or you can decide to stick your face in it. Now, you decide to pick the second option (I'm not here to judge... but that was a very weird choice.)

You later realize that it was a really shitty (pun totally intended) decision you made. You can either blame the dog, the dog's owner, the school system or the current president. But no matter who you try to blame, it was actually your fault. You were presented with a really shitty opportunity and you decided to take it. Now you're somewhere you don't want to be and you're the only person to blame.

Guess what, it's the same way with our traditional, mediocre way of doing things. We get offered this degree, job and late retirement game plan. If we decide to follow that plan, we will have to live with the results and we cannot blame others.

Now, there is nothing wrong with having a normal job with just a few vacations a year and then, hopefully, one day affording a nice retirement. Absolutely nothing. However, I am talking to the people who want more out of life. The people who want to travel the world and see everything. The ones who want to be world-class people living life to the fullest. I'm talking to the ones who have a desire for more and who are ready to do whatever it takes to get there. To those people, I have this very important message that I want you to live by:

Don't put your head in the massive dog excrement.

Chapter Bullet Points:

- Being realistic is a great way to suck at life.

- Most people live up to just 2% of their potential emotionally, mentally, physically, and financially.

- Money is a huge part of freedom and freedom is a huge part of happiness. With freedom, we can take care of our health, we can travel, and we can overall enjoy the good stuff life has to offer. This is difficult when money is an issue.

- The vast majority of people have a mediocre mindset. You can't let them influence you. The moment you give up on your dreams because a mediocre person told you to, you've lost.

- Spend time with ambitious, positive, and game-changing people. Your life will change in no time. (You can do this by joining the Cure Mediocrity Facebook group. Just saying.)

- Don't do what everybody else is doing because everybody is not living the life you want.

- Following the *traditional* way of doing things is perfectly fine. Just make sure this road will take you where you want to go.

- Life is 3% circumstances and 97% what you make of it.

PART 2:
THE CURE FOR
MEDIOCRITY

You've been brainwashed to believe that your dreams are *unrealistic* and *unacquirable*. However, you need to realize *everything* is possible. You could multiply your current dreams by a hundred and it would still be possible to achieve them, with the right mindset.

It can be very difficult to be taught, even programmed, to think one thing and then suddenly shift your entire belief system. **But you have to realize that as long as we don't *believe* our dreams are possible, they never will be.**

> *"He who says he can and he who says he can't are both usually right." - Confucius*

I remember when I thought becoming successful was impossible. I would look at athletes, artists, entrepreneurs, etc. and I would think: *They're different. I don't have these opportunities. Only a select few have these lucky opportunities and possibilities to achieve greatness.* Success seemed so out of reach and so esoteric. These beliefs were holding me down and keeping me from chasing more than mediocrity.

"Greatness is not this wonderful, esoteric, elusive, god-like feature that only the special among us will ever taste. It's something that truly exists in all of us." - Will Smith

When I started to realize my true potential and my endless possibilities, something happened. Life opened up in a way it never had before. I started feeling invincible and I started to feel like I could achieve whatever I wanted to. *THIS* is the mindset you want to build and grow. With this mindset, everything and anything is possible! The only limits you have are the ones you set for yourself.

[3]

WHY ARE YOU HERE?

Why are you here? What can you contribute to the world that no one else can? What are your unique attributes? What are your unique skills? Your passions?

Very few people can answer these questions. That's understandable because it can be very difficult and complicated to figure these things out.

What you need to realize, though, is that self-awareness is one of the most crucial parts of massive success and a world-class lifestyle. You need to know what your strengths are and what you suck at. You need to know what you love doing and what you hate doing. If you don't take advantage of the things that no one but you can do, you're leaving a lot of opportunities on the table.

> *"Self-awareness: When you know who you are, everything changes." -Gary Vaynerchuk*
>
> *"Self-awareness is the most important thing you can do to impact success." -Gary Vaynerchuk again. This guy is really into self-awareness!*

I realize that self-awareness might seem like this intangible, strange thing. That's what I thought the first hundred times I heard about it. Eventually, I started to see how crucial it actually was to know who we are. I started focusing on it and I immediately saw the effects. **Whatever you want to achieve in life, self-awareness is the key.**

WHO ARE YOU?

To understand who you are, you must know what your attributes, skills and passions are. You must know your strengths and weaknesses. Knowing these things about yourself is the first step toward success and fulfillment. Trust me, it's more important than you think it is.

Let's start with your passion. What does it mean to be passionate about something? The dictionary says passion is a strong or extravagant fondness, enthusiasm or desire for something. It's something that truly excites you and that you want to spend a lot of time on.

What are you passionate about? How do you like to spend your time? If you were to spend 16 hours a day on something for five years, what would that be? Ask yourself questions like that until you find out what you're truly passionate about.

Some great questions to ask yourself include: If I had all the money and all the time in the world, what would I be doing? How would I spend my time? Would I help others? How so?

I asked myself these questions when I wanted to figure out what my passion was. My answer was to study success. I would study wealth; who becomes wealthy and who becomes poor? I would study happiness; why are some people happy and fulfilled, while others feel stressed and depressed?

I realized that if I could do whatever I wanted whenever I wanted, I would study, educate myself, grow, improve and develop myself every minute from when I woke up until I went to bed. I'm the happiest when I'm learning new things that can improve my life. Whether that's improving my health, how I handle my money, my business, etc. Growing and learning is fun and, to be honest, I feel like I'm wasting every minute I'm not growing somehow. So, by asking myself these questions, I found that my passion was to learn about things that can improve lives.

Unfortunately, it's not enough to be passionate about something. You have to connect it to a skill. You might be passionate about playing League of Legends, catching javelins (yes, that's a thing) or doing handsprings, but if you can't connect it to a valuable skill, you will have a hard time making a living, much less becoming wealthy.

Combine something you love doing with something you're good at. When you have a combination of a passion and a skill, you'll love what you do and you'll be valuable to the world.

Most people lack one of these. They're either doing something they love but really suck at, or they're doing something they hate but do well. This is why people so often burn out.

So, what are you good at? What are your unique traits? With traits, I'm not just talking about being good at tennis or badminton. I'm talking about skills like being good with people. Having a strong, logical way of thinking. Being creative. Being innovative. Being a problem solver. Being a teacher.

Skills like these are where true value lies because everyone can become good at tennis, but not everyone can be a creative, innovative thinker. You need to realize what your skills are. And don't you dare throw something like, man, I don't have skills like that, at me. **We all have greatness within us - we just need to find it.** Self-awareness is key.

Finding your unique skills can be very difficult. I remember when I was told to find and be aware of my skills. It was incredibly challenging. So, how do you know what your skills are? Well, you need to ask people who will be brutally honest with you. This can be yourself or it can be family or friends.

It can sometimes be difficult to notice our own skills and traits. For this reason, it can be very beneficial to ask the people closest to you. I went up to the people who knew me best and I said something like this:

I've realized that there's something I really want to know about myself. I don't know if I'm capable of answering these questions myself. I need an outside perspective. It's very important that you're extremely honest while answering the following questions. Please do not hesitate to tell me the truth because only the truth will help me. Will you do me this favor? So, here are my questions: What are my key skills/attributes? What can I do that no one else can? If I were to become the best in the world at something, what would that be? Which skill or attribute do you think about when you hear my name?

I did this and I found that I was an extremely fast learner. People can walk me through some kind of process and I will understand it immediately because I see the logic. I can then easily implement what I learn into my life. When I realized this, I started to see that this is one of my strengths and it always has been. As a child, when my karate instructor taught us a new technique, I would understand and implement it immediately. When my instructors in other sports taught me new things to improve my game, I would implement it that same day. Same thing when I grew older. I could read a chapter of a book and I would immediately understand the concept and be able to implement it in my life. This is the only reason I did well in school. Trust me, it was not because of the dedication (there was just about zero of that).

The second skill I found was something I would've never noticed if I hadn't asked the people around me. My friends and family told me that I was good at explaining intangible, abstract concepts and turning them into simple principles that were easy to implement.

So, I had to combine my passion (growing as a person and learning things that will improve my life in some way) with my skills (learning advanced concepts in a fast and effective way + explaining things and turning advanced concepts into easy-to-understand principles).

I realized I can quickly and effectively study things that can improve lives and then turn those things into something everyone can take action on and implement. As you can see, combining passion and skill can be very powerful!

Now you have to find yours.

WHO NEEDS YOU?

When you have your passion and you have your skills, you need to find people who can benefit from your combination. Who can you help? Who has the problem that you have the solution for?

You see, so many people fuck up because they can't answer these questions. They just follow their passion without thinking about the fact that there needs to be a need for what you can do. **The reason so many businesses don't succeed is because they fail to fill a need.** This is why I hate advice like, just do what you love and success will be inevitable. Advice like this sets so many people up for failure.

Yes, you obviously need to be passionate and happy about what you're doing. That's a given. However, **if no one needs what you're doing, it doesn't matter how passionate you are.** You need to be able to improve other people's lives by doing what you want to do.

Combine passion, skill, and a fillable need and you will have your vehicle to success.

The people I can help with my passion + skills are hungry young people. People who want to do more than live a mediocre life. People who are tired of being lied to by society when it comes to wealth, success and happiness. So, the people I'm focusing on are hungry, dedicated people with a desire for the extraordinary lifestyle. They are often between 16 and 30 years old; these people make up my target audience.

I know I can help these people. I know I can provide life-changing ideas to help my target audience achieve the world-class lifestyle they desire. I also feel like someone has to tell the truth about society and the system. Our younger generation will grow up brainwashed and set up for mediocrity. Someone has to change that. Honestly, I don't think a lot of people will step forward and be honest like I am in this book. This means there's a massive need for my passion + skill combination.

How do you know if there's a need for your solution? How do you know if there are people out there who could benefit from what you can contribute? How do you know who your target audience is?

Well, one of my mentors taught me a great exercise for this. Doing this exercise will give you a clear idea about who you want to help.

First, create a fictional person. A character who would benefit from your passion + skill combination. Give the person a name, age, gender, work status, political view, income level, religion, hobby, education, social media preference, dreams, problems, etc. Craft the person to be the best possible customer you could sell your passion + skill combination to.

This exercise is extremely useful for 2 very important reasons:

It will show you if there's an audience you can contribute to. If you can create a fictional, but realistic, person who would benefit greatly from what you want to do, then there's probably a market for your passion + skill combination. Yay!

It will be a lot easier for you to find customers when you have a target audience.

Here's an example:

Name: Bob

Age: 43

Income level: $43,000

Marital status: Married

Children: 2

Etc.

The more detailed the better. Do not commit to anything without knowing if there's an actual need for what you can offer.

MASTER IT

When you know what your unique skills and passions are and you know who can benefit from them, your next step is to become as good as possible at helping those people. Become the best at improving their lives. Master your craft.

"The more you learn, the more you earn." - Warren Buffett

The better you are at your craft, the better you will be at improving your customers' lives. The better you are at improving your customers' lives, the more valuable you are to them. The more valuable you are to your customers, the more you will be able to help people, which is an amazing and fulfilling feeling. And the more you can help people, the more you get paid. So, as you can see, being good at your craft is a huge win in many ways.

It is, for this reason, crucial that you always learn, improve and work on your craft. Always find new ways to improve and become better at solving your customers' problems. The reason someone like Tony Robbins can take a six-figure number for a single 1-on-1 session is because he's the best there is at what he does. The better you become at your craft and the more you learn, the more you will be able to achieve. Always improve.

Now, there are three different ways to improve at something. They're all very effective and they all provide different benefits and results.

1. Studying. The first way of learning is to study. Studying is the application of the mind to the acquisition of knowledge, as by reading, investigation or reflection. This way of learning is extremely crucial and very effective. By studying, you can learn about the results of a technique or method without having to experiment with it yourself. You can learn something in 10 seconds that would've taken you 10 years to find out on your own. This is possible because other people have done what you're trying to do.

Now, there's a lot of different ways to study. Books are my absolute favorite because you can learn so much from them. It doesn't matter which topic you want to improve at, some expert has written a book about it. Books are amazing. Another way to study is through seminars and webinars. These are also very valuable. And then, of course, there's always studying materials like blogs, magazines, YouTube videos, podcasts, etc.

Regardless of your studying preference, you have to do it consistently and frequently. If you're not constantly learning and improving, then you're falling behind because your competitors are. The next two ways of learning will not work if you don't study. If you want to master your craft, you have to study. If you want to make an impact and become wealthy, you have to master your craft. Studying is crucial.

2. Practicing. Studying is crucial because it provides knowledge. But, contrary to the famous quote, knowledge is not power. Far from it, actually. Knowledge is potential power. With knowledge, you can decide to stash it somewhere in your brain and never use it. This way, it will not be very powerful. However, you can also decide to apply it and implement it in your life. This is when knowledge becomes extremely powerful.

"Knowing is not enough, we must apply." - Bruce Lee

Practicing is how you take that potential power and turn it into results. As you can see, it's hard to practice anything if you don't have the knowledge and if you don't know what to do. It is also useless to study if you never practice any of it because you can't implement it. **Studying and practicing is a powerful combo that will make you very valuable to the marketplace.**

I'm not gonna go further into practicing because we all know how to practice something. It's just doing it over and over again while trying to do better every time.

3. Modeling. The third way of learning is through modeling...and I'm not talking about becoming a runway model. What I mean by modeling is that you should model people who have done what you want to do, or folks who at least know how to get you there. You can do this through a mentor, offline or online.

So, which one of these three should you use to improve on your craft? All of them. They all work together and they all supplement each other. Do these as much as possible, preferably daily, because you will become so much more valuable. Remember, the more you learn, the more you earn. So, if you continue to improve, you will continue to be paid more.

SELL IT

Good work is about providing value, making an impact and changing people's lives. However, you cannot do that without making money. You will not have the resources to do all these things if you don't have an income. This is why it is so crucial to monetize your skill.

Now, there are two different ways of doing this. Two completely different roads. The road you decide to take will have a lot to say when it comes to your future success or mediocrity. With the first road, you have no limitations. You will have the opportunity to change the world. With the other road, you will have the opportunity to be a slave. Unfortunately, most people pick the latter. This means they will live in mediocrity instead of their desired, world-class lifestyle. This road offers no freedom.

Be careful when choosing between these two roads because with one of them, you're building your dream. With the other, you're building someone else's.

What's the road that leads to mediocrity and no freedom? It's relying 100% on a job. This is the way a lot of people decide to be paid for their skills and effort. Well, that's not true. Actually, they get paid for their time. For every hour we work in a job, we get paid.

However, with only 24 hours in a day, there is a limit on what you can get paid when you're trading time for money. Trading time for money is not efficient or scalable, and doesn't provide any freedom. I'll talk about these things later in the book, though.

> *"If you work for a living, you're trading time for money. Frankly, it's just about the worst trade you can make. Why? Because you can always get more money but you can't get more time." - Tony Robbins*

With a job, you're only getting paid when you're working. The second you stop working, you stop making money. This is why the only people making excellent amounts of money in a job are the ones who work 60-80 hours a week.

This is why I wouldn't call doctors, lawyers, etc. rich. Heck, when you divide their salary by the number of hours they work, they're actually sometimes making less than the average jobs. Does this sound like a recipe for greatness, prosperity, fulfillment and freedom? Nah... it sounds like a recipe for security, security and security... until something happens to your company, the market or maybe even your health. If you get fired or lose the ability to work, where's your sweet security?

Please realize that, unless you want to wait until you're in a wheelchair, having a job will not make you wealthy alone and it will definitely not provide freedom. Even if you lower your monthly expenses by not drinking your daily $5 Starbucks coffee.

Now, a job can be a great tool for building wealth, if you use it right. More on that later, though.

Only 4% of workers believe they'll be able to retire at age 55. Think about that. Best case scenario, if you're a part of the 4%, you'll retire before age 55. These statistics are extremely eye-opening compared to the number of twenty-somethings who retired by following a different road. Here's a fact more about how amazing relying on a job is: 80% of workers aged 30-54 believe they won't have enough money stored away when retiring.

What's the second road? God, I'm so glad you asked. As some of you probably guessed, it's entrepreneurship.

CHAPTER BULLET POINTS:

- Self-awareness is key. Know your strengths and know your weaknesses.

- Passion is a necessity but it's not enough. We need to combine it with a valuable skill.

- Greatness is within all of us. We just have to find it and use it.

- We must then find a need that we can fill with our passion + skill combination. If there isn't a need for our solution, it will never matter how passionate we are.

- Master your craft. The better you are, the more valuable you will be to your customers. This means you'll help more people and make more money in the process.

- Sell your solution to people who can benefit from it. You can do this through a job or for yourself.

[4]

ENTREPRENEURSHIP

You know who you are, what your skills and passions are, and who you can help. When you know these things, it's time to monetize it and create an impact. Yes, you can do this through a job. However, there is another road you should consider.

Imagine building something that helps millions around the planet. Imagine you getting wealthy as fuck. Both these things happen without your presence. It happens while you sleep, eat or travel. You will, because of this, have extreme freedom like you've never imagined possible. Live a few tough years doing a lot of hard work and you will live the rest of your life like a king.

Wait, is this some kind of alternate universe? Some kind of imaginary reality? Well, it's actually called entrepreneurship and it's the only way to live life fully on *your* terms. Tell me this doesn't sound appealing.

Entrepreneurship is the main part of *The Cure for Mediocrity*. Now, entrepreneurship is not for everybody. Not everyone is built for this way of living. However, I really think that everyone should experience it in some way. The amazing possibilities that come with entrepreneurship are way too good to not give it at least one try.

You don't have to be born with god-like abilities and talents to become an entrepreneur. You don't have to be one in a million to have this amazing opportunity. The reason so many people hesitate about becoming entrepreneurs is because they think they need to be the next Mark Zuckerberg or Steve Jobs. I've been there, trust me. I thought becoming an entrepreneur would require me to code the next social media app. Or that I had to raise $5 million worth of capital.

This is not the case. You really do not have to have a billion-dollar idea to get started.

I looked at my friends, my family and strangers and I asked myself, why isn't anyone an entrepreneur? It really confused me because, to me, entrepreneurship seemed like the greatest thing ever. So, I decided to ask them; I asked them *why* they weren't entrepreneurs.

The following were the most common answers I received:

- Never thought about it. (There's a lack of awareness about entrepreneurship.)

- Didn't know how. (Lack of entrepreneurial education.)

- Didn't have a great, billion-dollar idea.

- I'm not capable of doing something like that.

It's really a shame that so many people miss this opportunity because they think they aren't capable of doing it. I don't want this to happen to you. I want you to know that you don't have to invent the next piece of technology to become an entrepreneur. You really don't!

In the previous chapter, we talked about your skills and your passion. We also talked about filling a need that other people have. This is the perfect foundation for a business. If you can make one person pay one dollar for you to use your skill to make his or her life better, then you're an entrepreneur. You don't need a website (even though you can make one for free very easily these days). You don't need a physical product, and you certainly do not need some kind of warehouse or a huge office. It really doesn't take much to get started.

I'm going to talk a little bit more about the different ways of running a business. For now, though, just realize that everyone, including you and your friends, can start a business, become an entrepreneur and start building something great. Right now I'd like to tell you a little bit more about the benefits of entrepreneurship.

So, *why is entrepreneurship so freaking awesome?* God, I'm so glad you asked. Entrepreneurship is awesome for many reasons. One of the main things I love about it is that I can live my life exactly how I want to. I can literally craft the perfect day and then live it. Now *that's* freedom.

Another thing I love about entrepreneurship is that there are no limitations (especially if you pay attention to the next chapter). You can always do more. You can always earn more, give more, be more, create more, etc. There's absolutely no ceiling on what you can accomplish. The sky is not even the limit when you're an entrepreneur, you work hard, and you follow the three ingredients in the next chapter.

The third, and probably the most important reason that I like entrepreneurship is that you get to help others. Now, I know there are many jobs that really make a difference and improve people's lives. I really appreciate people working those jobs. However, when you're an entrepreneur, you can help people on a much larger scale.

Doctors, lawyers, and psychologists are all extremely important people with really helpful professions. I respect that a lot. However, it can be hard to impact millions of people. These professions allow you to help one person at a time, which is great. With entrepreneurship, though, you can help *millions* of people.

You can't help a million people by helping one at a time.

IT'S NOT ALL SUNSHINE AND RAINBOWS

Now, I make entrepreneurship sound like one big fairy tale. This is not the case. Entrepreneurship isn't all easy. It's a lot of blood, sweat and tears. Especially in the beginning. It requires a lot of work and it requires many sacrifices. Starting a business is really simple, but it takes a lot of work to get it up and running.

Depending on how much you want to succeed, you'll have to sacrifice some things. You'll have to sacrifice some of the parties. You'll have to sacrifice time-wasting activities like social media, TV, etc. The first couple of years will require you to focus on your business and to really prioritize that.

In some cases, you might even have to cut friendships if they are dragging you down and preventing you from succeeding. I've had to do this with a lot of my friends. Simply because they were on completely different paths and they would influence me negatively, trying to pull me away from my dreams. One moment I'd be extremely motivated about what I was doing; I'd be *in the zone.* Then, I'd hang out with some friends who would try to encourage me to drop everything to party more.

It's not fun making this kind of decisions. However, not long after I started my entrepreneurial lifestyle, I realized that those sacrifices were required. There's no way around them.

Fortunately, I was (and still am) strong enough to focus on the bigger picture. I was delayed-gratification-oriented, which is when you prioritize long-term pleasure over short-term pleasure. If you want to succeed as an entrepreneur, or in life in general, you have to be delayed-gratification-oriented and focus on the long-term thinking. This can definitely be difficult and extremely challenging. It's a requirement for success and wealth, though.

Earlier in this chapter, I was talking about the fact that everyone can become an entrepreneur. What I meant by that is that everyone has the opportunity to start a small business. It really doesn't take much to get started. However, it takes a lot of time and work to build that small business into something great that will produce enough income for you to thrive for the rest of your life.

So, yeah, everyone can start a business and everyone should at least taste entrepreneurship. It is not hard to get started but it will require hard work and sacrifices to really turn it into something amazing that provides you the freedom you want. It is *so* worth it.

The Reward

Entrepreneurship may require a lot of hard work and sacrifices. However, it is 11000% worth it. If you can survive the startup period, which is usually anywhere from six to thirty months, you will be rewarded immensely. I don't think any entrepreneur regrets the hard work and the sacrifices. I do, however, think that when mediocre people look at the results and the rewards, they regret not becoming entrepreneurs. Everyone wants the reward, the amazing lifestyle, but few are willing to pay the price, the hard work.

"Eat shit for 24 months and eat caviar for the rest of your life." - Gary Vaynerchuk

Entrepreneurship is worth it and there are so many reasons for that. First of all, you'll get a sense of achievement and pride. This feeling will boost your confidence to levels you could've never imagined. You'll be so proud that you've created something that improves other people's lives. The fact that you can do something that other people will pay actual money for in exchange is invaluable.

Also, with all the money you have the opportunity to make as an entrepreneur, you will be able to give so much more. Imagine being able to invite your entire family on a nice vacation. Imagine being able to buy your best friend or your brother a brand new car for his birthday. And then, of course, imagine being able to feed hundreds, thousands or maybe even millions of starving children. This feeling of improving other people's lives is incredible and it's what keeps me extremely motivated.

Trust me when I say that the hard work that comes with starting a business is worth it. Entrepreneurship is very rewarding and you will not regret it, ever.

What if I fail, though? Well, this might sound cliché and cheesy. But, in my opinion, you can either win or you can learn. Giving entrepreneurship a shot is a win no matter what happens. The way I see it, if giving entrepreneurship a shot will eliminate all kinds of future *what if* thoughts, then wasting 4, 8 or 12 months is still a huge win.

If you fail, you'll have learned a ton about entrepreneurship and about yourself. If you succeed, you will forever live the life you've always dreamed of.

I dropped out of school at age 16 to pursue my entrepreneurial dreams. Best decision of my life, by the way. Was I afraid of failing and being ridiculed? Afraid of not making it work and having to go back to school? *Absolutely.* However, I decided to look at it differently. I thought about the worst case and the best case scenarios.

This is what I realized:

Worst case scenario. I drop out of school at age 16 to pursue my entrepreneurial dreams. Unfortunately, after seven months of hard work and persistence, I realize that this isn't for me. I will have learned so many things that no traditional education would ever be able to teach me. Also, I would've learned a lot about myself. And here's the most important thing that would happen: Because I tried to chase my dreams, I will never have those nagging *what if* thoughts. I will never have regrets about not giving entrepreneurship a shot.

What do I do now? Is my life forever screwed? Nah man, I'm just gonna go back to school and call it a gap year. I would've had a fun, educational year. I will be done with all my schooling a year later than I otherwise would have.

Best case scenario. I drop out of school at age 16 to pursue my entrepreneurial dream. It's fun, it's exciting and I find that I'm actually pretty good at it. After a few months of working hard, I have built something that helps a ton of people and I'm making a killing in the process. This gives me the ability to travel and spend my time exactly how I want at a young age.

What do I do now? I live the rest of my life exactly how I want to. I keep scaling my business to build an amazing legacy. I give a lot of my resources to help the people I love. I do a lot of charity work too. This boosts my confidence and my self-esteem like nothing else.

When you look at it this way, can you see why my fears and my doubts suddenly vanished? Worst case scenario is barely a bad thing. Best case scenario is living the dream. Now tell me it's not worth giving a shot!

I don't know if I've talked enough about the fact that entrepreneurship is great. So, here's more about it. *Enjoy.*

You help a ton of people and you make a massive impact. Because of this, you'll make a ton of money. Because of this, you will have incredible freedom. You will have no limits and you'll be able to live life on your terms.

You see, I've talked a lot about how starting a business comes with a lot of hard work. What you have to realize, however, is that everything you sacrifice in the startup period will come back multiplied, *by a lot.*

Sacrifice some of the lame parties at your friend's house today, and you'll be able to invite your friends to amazing parties all over the globe in a few years. Sacrifice that expensive pair of shoes today and you'll be able to buy 100 pairs later. Spend your money on your business today instead of the newest gadget and you will be able to get all the gadgets for yourself, and everyone else, later. If you work hard and you sacrifice right now to build your business, the rewards will come back even greater.

This is the delayed vs instant gratification thing I was talking about earlier. If you can suffer a little bit of short-term pain today, you'll enjoy long-term pleasure later. This, by the way, works with everything else in life too. Sacrifice the cheeseburger in the present and you'll enjoy long-term energy, confidence and good health. Delayed gratification will always win against instant gratification.

So, yeah, I would definitely be lying if I said entrepreneurship was all easy. Even though it's easy to begin, it can be hard to scale and grow a business. It requires a lot of work in the early phases. You have to realize, though, that it is 100% worth it. It's also the only way you can live life completely on your terms.

How Do I Start, Though?

By now, you should be pretty much sold, or at least interested, in taking a shot at this amazing thing called entrepreneurship. But where to begin? At first, it can seem very overwhelming and complicated to start a business.

Now, obviously the level of complication depends on the kind of business you decide to start. A new product invention might take two years while a consulting business might only take two hours to start. Just like there are many ways to have a job, there are also a ton of ways to be an entrepreneur and run a business. I'd need more than one book if I were to talk about all of them, though.

Here, I'm not gonna help you find the perfect business idea. That's simply not possible for me to do in a single book. I may create a course for that in the future, though. If you want help with finding the perfect business to start, contact me and maybe I can personally help you.

The reason I can't help you find your perfect business in *this book* is because there's no one-size-fits-all business that everyone should start. And, since there are a lot of different people reading this book, I would hate to suggest only one method of doing things. It simply wouldn't work.

Instead, I'm going to show you the main categories of businesses that you can start. You have to realize, though, that under each of these categories, there are a million different ways of doing things. You'll have to pick one you find interesting and then research it further. Again, if I were to guide you completely in this decision, it would not be through a book.

Let's quickly go over some business ideas:

1. Physical products.

This is, without a doubt, the most advanced. If you have an idea for a product that can solve some kind of problem, then this is a business you could look into. I usually suggest that businesses like these are for more experienced entrepreneurs, though. But yeah, if this is what you wanna do, then go ahead. Start by researching product development and study the process from idea to product manufacturing.

2. Information products.

This is a great way to start. I actually got started with this model. It is extremely easy to get started and this is why I think most "newbies" should try this. You want to create some kind of course that teaches your customers something. Let's say you want to create a course about learning Spanish. You can then create some kind of file that people can download. This will be like a mini book but it often has videos and images included too. Bonus points if you can create action steps for your customers to take action on after they've gone through the course.

Finally, you can sell your course for your preferred price on Udemy, an online learning platform, or you can sell them on your own website. Don't have a website? Creating one is really simple these days; you can have one up and running in minutes.

3. Selling other people's products.

Another thing you can do is sell other people's products for a commission. This is called *affiliate marketing*. The way it works is that the company you want to sell for will give you a unique link with your ID. Every time someone clicks that link and buys something on the website, you get a commission. This can be everything from 3% to 95% of the revenue you created for the company. Let's say you send me a link to some random product that's selling for $55. If I buy it, you get a 35% commission. I click that link and I buy the product. Slam bam, you just made $19.25!

Affiliate marketing is a very easy way to get started. In the future, I'm going to have an affiliate program you can join, if you're interested. I'm working on it.

4. Selling attention.

To make money selling attention, you have to have some kind of following. Say you have 100k followers on Instagram. Then Nike pays you to make a video promoting their shoes. It's pretty simple and it's a very lucrative business... when you have the following. A lot of companies want to get in front of 100k followers. However, building that kind of following is a lot easier said than done.

If you're interested in doing YouTube videos, building an Instagram following or growing a huge Facebook following, you can try this business model.

5. Consulting.

If you know a lot about a specific topic, you can choose to do consulting. Consulting is giving expert advice about something you're better at than your customer or client. Create a small website that explains who you are, what you can do for your clients, and how they can contact you.

A lot of consultants do one-hour sessions. If you feel like you and your skills can take a person from one place to a better place in his or her life with a one-hour session, then consulting might be your way to go.

6. Speeches.

Take everything you know about a specific topic. Now, craft a speech out of it! Reach out to schools, communities, companies, etc. and see if anyone is interested in listening to what you have to say.

If you have some kind of message that you just have to share with the world and that you feel can bring true value to the audience's life, then starting a speaking career might not be a bad idea.

7. Book.

Writing a book. This is really a great way to explode your life as an entrepreneur. If you write a valuable book and you market it correctly, it will be one of the most amazing tools to have as an entrepreneur.

You can use it to gain credibility so that people will look at you as someone who knows what he/she is talking about. You're not going to make a lot of money with books because they're so low-priced. You can, however, make a lot of money *because of* a book. A book will make people hire you as their consultant or as a speaker. A book will make people buy your future products.

If you feel like you have something to share, and you like the idea of writing a book, then I definitely think you should go ahead and do it.

CONCLUSION

If you're not an entrepreneur yet, then I hope these business models gave you some ideas about how to get started. I hope you started thinking about what you want to do and what choices you'd make regarding business and entrepreneurship. A way of doing things that fits your passions, skills and your personality. I'm sorry I couldn't go into further details with the individual business models. You can contact me if you want further guidance and assistance on picking the right business model for you.

If you're already an entrepreneur, then I hope you realize that you can still take advantage of some of these business models. You see, I'm engaged in all of them. It's never bad to have multiple streams of income. In fact, the average millionaire has 7 different income streams. I know that you, as an experienced entrepreneur, might have heard about them all already. I challenge you to find a way to add an additional stream of income within the next 90 days.

The next chapter will be extremely valuable for everyone, whether you are already an entrepreneur or not. Entrepreneurship is a part of *The Cure for Mediocrity*, but it is nothing without the three ingredients I'll be talking about in the next chapter. You see, the majority of entrepreneurs are still super mediocre.

The Cure for Mediocrity is entrepreneurship with the three ingredients I'll be talking about in next chapter. Pay close attention because, if you don't, you might end up mediocre. We don't want that.

CHAPTER BULLET POINTS:

- Most people don't get started in entrepreneurship because they think they need a billion-dollar idea.

- Entrepreneurship is very simple but it's far from easy. Success as an entrepreneur requires sacrifices and hard work.

- Entrepreneurship is great for many reasons and everyone should experience it in some way.

- Building a business is hard work but it's worth it.

- Many entrepreneurs are still mediocre. To prevent this happening to you, pay close attention to the next chapter.

[5]

THE THREE INGREDIENTS

Entrepreneurship is definitely the right way to achieve the freedom and the lifestyle a lot of us desire. With entrepreneurship, we can achieve extraordinary results and accomplish great things. I don't think I need to talk more about how great entrepreneurship is, though. At this point, I think most people have noticed my passion for entrepreneurship.

Entrepreneurship is just amazing for creating success and wealth.

So, every entrepreneur will become a multimillionaire, *right?* Every business owner is extremely wealthy, *right?* We all know this isn't true. There are tons of entrepreneurs and business owners who have even less freedom than normal job owners. Because, you see, there are a lot of ways to do entrepreneurship wrong. This will result in greater mediocrity than having a normal job.

But why? Why are some businesses worth hundreds of millions while others are worth absolutely nothing? Why are some entrepreneurs multi-millionaires while others are slaves to their stupid businesses? Is it because of luck? Because of their level of skills?

Actually, the difference is not any of those things. It's because of three crucial ingredients. If you lack one of them, you'll have a hard time building anything great. Without these three ingredients, you will have a ton of limitations, which means you can still be mediocre even though you are a business owner.

You see, the reason a job can't make you wealthy alone is because of its mathematical limitations. There are so many boundaries when you have a job. So many things that limit your capabilities and your possibilities. Unfortunately, a lot of businesses have these limitations too. They will, for this reason, not have the opportunities to do great things, ever.

So, instead of being a slave working 8 hours a day, they work 12. Instead of working 5 days to get a 2 day weekend, they work in 6:1 or 7:0 ratios. They are slaves to their businesses and they're even more mediocre than the average worker.

The business owner will keep doing this, hoping that someday the business will explode and he can retire. What he doesn't realize, however, is that it never will. He has set his business up for mediocrity by not adding the three ingredients to his business. As long as he doesn't change his business model to include these crucial ingredients, he will never be able to achieve his dream lifestyle. Instead of building a system, he's become a slave who trades time for money just like normal workers.

The worst part about all this is that the business owner will continue trying for sometimes 20-30 years. He has no idea why he isn't wealthy. He'll start to think that business is about luck and that he just wasn't meant to be successful. What would've saved him 20 wasted years? If he had started his business with these three ingredients, or at least implemented them later on. But he doesn't know about these ingredients because he's not reading and educating himself.

This is why I want you to know that I really respect you for reading this book. I respect that you're so dedicated to success that you commit to educating yourself and really learning about the things you need to know. Trust me, by educating yourself on the important things in life, you'll have a huge competitive advantage over those who don't. Keep educating yourself like this and you will achieve great things.

Before diving into the three crucial ingredients for business and entrepreneurship, I want you to realize that what I'm about to talk about is the reason why so few people succeed and live life completely on their terms while others are slaves.

Now, everything in this book contributes to *The Cure for Mediocrity*. Every single sentence is an important part, and everything in this book will help you achieve the lifestyle you want and live life completely on your own terms. However, it's safe to say that entrepreneurship combined with these three ingredients are definitely the main part.

Let's dive in.

1. CONTROL

The first ingredient is control. In a regular job, no one has any kind of control. Unfortunately, a lot of businesses don't have control either. There are so many people trying to become wealthy in an environment they cannot control. This is a very bad way to do things.

You can choose to put your success and finances in other people's hands and let them have complete control over you, or you can decide to learn from other people and then take control yourself. You can decide to depend on third parties, or you can decide to rely on your own work-ethic, skills and results. Choose the second option.

"There is no dependence that can be sure but a dependence on one's self." - John Gay

To fully control of your life, you have to be *in control* of your life. This may sound weird and stupid but I actually felt pretty genius when I came up with this. Because there are so many mediocre people walking around feeling in complete control over their lives, yet they're so dependent on the job market, the housing market, the stock market, etc. You can't be in control of your life when there are so many important variables that you can't control. It's simply not possible.

There are way too many people who feel like they're in complete control while they really aren't. For so many people, if they lose their job, they're screwed. If their house decreases in value, they're screwed. If something happens to the stock market, there goes their retirement.

I'm here to tell you that if you rely on a ton of third parties, like the job market, then you're in great danger because you can't control third parties.

The reason I call having a job *Just Over Broke* is because, at any given time, someone can fire you and you'll be broke. Someone can literally, within a second, take away your job and therefore your income. Your entire life is in other people's hands.

These people can take it all away from you whenever they want to and there's nothing you can do about it. That's what I call secure lol.

So, how does all this translate to business?

Well, a lot of businesses rely on third parties too. Let me give you a few examples:

A franchisee: The franchisor has complete control over the franchisee.

A retailer with only a few brands. If the company whose products you're selling decides to change or eliminate the product you're selling, you've just lost a huge part of your business and your revenue.

Every business with only one income stream. There are lots of things that can ruin an income stream. So, if you only have one, then you're in great danger, you have no control and you could potentially be ruined soon.

"Think manufacture, not retail." - MJ DeMarco

Now, I'm not saying that every retailer (someone selling other people's products) is completely out of control. It's cool to have a clothing shop with 40 different brands. This way, if something happens to one of the brands, you're not ruined. You might not even notice it.

Unfortunately, a lot of retailers depend on one or two companies. Imagine if a clothing shop sold clothes from just two or three brands. Then, one of the brands decides to switch business models, or maybe even cut the entire relationship. The retailer is now absolutely fucked because there goes a huge part of his product line. Imagine if Walmart only sold products from two different manufactures. Then, one of the manufacturers decides to change things and it cuts Walmart off. Walmart just lost billions of revenue and would probably go bankrupt.

It can also be as simple as the manufacturer raising its prices a little bit. This would make all of your products have smaller margins, which could potentially put you out of business.

So, if you decide to become a retailer, or any other kind of business, it is extremely important that you make sure nothing can break you like that. If someone can do that, then you're not in control.

The way you do this is to A) sell your own products, or B) have a wide variety of manufacturers so that it wouldn't matter if one of them cuts you off or changed its methods. I like option A better because then you can decide what to sell, when to sell it and you get to decide your margins. Also, you won't be at risk for complete elimination unless you do it yourself. Again, like John Gay said, there is no dependence that can be sure but a dependence on one's self.

You need to be in complete control over your life and your business. You can only do this by controlling the important variables that shape your life. **You cannot change or improve anything that you can't control.** This is why you see workers with no control getting 3% pay raises while entrepreneurs in control enjoy 3000% pay raises.

Making sure you have this ingredient in your *Cure for Mediocrity* is also extremely beneficial when it comes to freedom. As you can imagine, having control is a huge part of freedom. With this ingredient, you can control when to do what, and how. Without this ingredient you'll not only be tossed around by third parties, you'll also be in great danger.

The first ingredient of *The Cure for Mediocrity* is control. To achieve the amazing lifestyle you desire, you need to be in complete control of your life and your business. This means that there cannot be any major variables out of your control. Make sure you have this ingredient in your life and business, and you will already be ahead of almost everyone else.

2. SCALABILITY

The next ingredient is *scalability*. This ingredient is what will determine your potential for wealth and success. With this ingredient, there's no limit on your capabilities. This is the ingredient that billion dollar companies have that small coffee shops don't. If your business can't scale, you'll forever be limited to mediocrity. If your business has the ability to scale, then you'll have absolutely *no limits.*

Unfortunately, a lot of businesses, almost all of them actually, are lacking this ingredient. It's what that sandwich place downtown is lacking. It's what your uncle's small plumbing service lacks. Overall, it's one of the reasons that small businesses are *small.*

MJ DeMarco describes this concept amazingly in his book *The Millionaire Fastlane.* He says that, in business, you can choose to play in the ocean or in a pool at the local park. This captures the concept of scalability perfectly. You can start your business in a pool, which means that you'll have no potential of true scalability, or you can start your business in the ocean, which means there'll be absolutely no limits for your success and wealth.

Unfortunately, far too many entrepreneurs and business owners are playing in the pool. This is why you see some people working on the same business for 15 years without becoming wealthy. There's no scalability which means there's no opportunity for the business to be great and achieve anything. This is such a shame because the business, if it was able to scale, could probably be huge and successful.

Even though you can always change your business model later, you should really put some thought and consideration into scalability as soon as possible. The longer it takes for you to think about scalability, the further you'll get down the wrong road with a dead end.

So, if you're not an entrepreneur yet, please don't start anything without reading this chapter and really thinking seriously about scalability.

If you're already an entrepreneur in business, you should really take a good, honest look at your business model and ask yourself if what you're doing is truly scalable. If it's not, you should probably adjust some things and turn it into something you can scale.

THE LAW OF EFFECTION

To really understand what scalability is, we have to understand the law of effection. Without it, we will never become wealthy. The law of effection is where so many businesses fail. They limit themselves by creating a business that can't impact enough people.

I first learned about this concept in MJ DeMarco's best-selling book *The Millionaire Fastlane.* It's genius.

If we want to make millions, we must make an impact equal to that. So, the more we impact people (positively, of course), the more money we make. The law of effection is what determines how big of an impact we can make, which translates to how much money we make. Because, as we all know, the more we help people, the more money we make.

The Law of Effection looks like this:

Impact = Reach (the amount of people we help) * Magnitude (the amount we help each person)

So, **the amount of money we make is determined by the amount of positive impact we have on other people's lives.** And the amount of impact we make is determined by the number of people we help multiplied by the amount/magnitude of how much we help them.

As you can probably guess, having a limit on either scale or magnitude will limit your opportunities to impact people, which will impact your money-making potential. So, if you want to get really wealthy, you cannot have limits on scale and magnitude. This is one of the biggest determinants of your future success in business and entrepreneurship.

We can also translate it into money: Income = Units sold * Unit profit

Again, this shows that if there's a limit on the number of units you can sell (reach) and there's a limit on the price (magnitude), then there's simply no possibility for wealth.

Think about the local sandwich shop. Does he have a limit on his reach? Absolutely. He can probably sell 50, 75 or maybe even 100 sandwiches a day. Not more, though, because he A) doesn't have that much time in a day and B) there's not enough customers for that. What about magnitude then? Well, he can probably raise his prices by $1.5 per sandwich. This will never make him rich, though. So, he has a limit on reach and he has a limit on magnitude. This guy will, under his current circumstances, never get wealthy no matter how long he works on his business.

What about the hairdresser who opened her own salon? Well, does she have a limit on the amount of people she can do daily? Absolutely. Does she have a limit on what she can do for that person? Definitely. She can have a finite number of customers and she has a limit on what she can charge for each customer. Under her current circumstances, she will not become wealthy with her salon.

A coffee shop is actually an unscalable, dead end business. There's a limited number of customers and there's a limited price on each cup of coffee. The owner will not achieve freedom and he will certainly not acquire wealth.

What about Starbucks, then? That is a great question, my friend. If coffee shops are so terrible, then how did Howard Schultz build Starbucks to a 10-figure company? Well, because Starbucks isn't a coffee shop. Starbucks is almost 30,000 coffee shops spread over 72 countries. Howard Schultz took a business from the local pool and moved it to the ocean.

Same thing with McDonald's, Burger King, Subway, etc. Subway isn't a sandwich place. Subway is almost 50,000 sandwich places. Again, this small, unscalable business exploded when they moved from the local pool to the ocean.

Both of these examples, Starbucks and Subway, prove that you can build huge businesses when you expand. And you can only expand when you have room to expand. You don't have room to expand when you're in the pool. You have to be in the ocean before you can expand with no limitations.

The pool is when you play locally. You're doing business in the pool if your only customers are the ones living within a few blocks radius. This will not make you wealthy. You're in the ocean if you can serve customers from all over the world. This has the potential you make you very, very wealthy.

Make sure that your business has the potential and the ability to go worldwide or at least all over your country. Also, try to not put a limit on the magnitude of which you can help them. So, instead of only having one product, try to have more. Have small products that every customer can use and then have some bigger products for the customers who need more than the small one. This way, you will eliminate the limit on how much you can help your individual customer.

I thought about scalability from the get-go. As some of you might know, I was born and raised in Denmark (du er sej hvis du oversætter dette på Google). Now, Denmark is a really small country with only six million inhabitants. I decided that I was not going to go all in on a business that had this kind of limitation. I knew that, eventually, the size of my country and the amount of people here would really limit my opportunities for success and wealth.

So, even though my English sucked when I first started out (it still does, to be honest), I decided that I was definitely going international. With the entire world as my playground, I would have much bigger possibilities and opportunities. I am so glad I made that decision back then.

You see, with this book, I can speak to someone in Australia, I can give some Turkish guy a new perspective on life and I can make an impact on someone from Mexico. Now *that* is reach. I can then decide to create additional products, or maybe even offer 1-on-1 coaching. This way, I will not only have unlimited reach, I will also increase the magnitude and the amount that I can help people. Because of this, I have no limit on the amount I can help people and on the impact I can make. Yay!

There are definitely some questions you need to ask yourself, regardless of you already being an entrepreneur or not. These questions will steer you in the right direction and they will make you aware of where you're going. It's a shame wasting 20 years of your life on an unscalable business just because you didn't ask yourself these questions:

- What's the ceiling on my reach? 2000 people? 200,000? 200,000,000?

- How much can I possibly help each individual?

- How much can I possibly make per customer? $35? $500? $20,000?

- Is my business capable of serving customers from all over the world?

- Why is Daniel Hauge so freaking awesome?

- Is my business capable of having franchises?

- Is my business truly scaleable overall?

Whether you're about to start your business or you've been in business for 57 years, ask yourself these questions. Because, if your business isn't scaleable, then you're wasting your time, energy and money. You and I are not interested in you wasting your time, energy and money.

3. TIME DETACHMENT

This is the last ingredient in what determines your future level of freedom. Some businesses require the owner to work 70 hours a week to survive, while some businesses make the owner money without him doing anything. What's the difference between these two? The difference is whether the business has this ingredient or not.

This extremely valuable, powerful and absolutely crucial ingredient is called *time detachment*. The ability to detach your time from your business. If you can't do that, then you'll forever be a slave. You will not set yourself up for freedom in the future without this important ingredient.

While it's perfectly normal to spend all your resources, money, time, energy, attention, focus etc. on building your business in the startup phase, it's not something I'd like to endure for 20, 30 or 40 years. I want my reward, *freedom*, at some point.

Unfortunately, some people stay in the startup phase for 40 years. They never seem to take time off to take a vacation or be with friends. They're working 70 hours a week and they've done this since they started the business. They're living below their means with an almost non-existing paycheck because, if they pay themselves, their business will lose money.

Why? Because they've set themselves up for mediocrity. They started a business without the ingredient of time detachment and, as a result, they're now forever trapped as slaves to businesses they hate. They're not capable of detaching their time from their business, thus leaving them in a situation where they only make money when they're at the office. If they don't spend all their time at their business, they lose it all.

This is a lot worse than having a normal job. When you have a job, you at least get your weekends and a proper salary. With a business where you can't detach your time, you'll work every single day just to survive.

Business with time detachment > Normal job > Business without time detachment.

Having the ingredient of time detachment means that your business can function without you physically being there. Your business should be able to make money and do exactly what it's supposed to do regardless of you being present or not. A chiropractor gets paid for every hour he spends with a client. A nightclub owner makes money whether he's at the club or sipping mojitos on the other side of the planet.

You need to detach your income from your time. **If you only get paid when you work, it's either a job or a very shitty business model.** If you build something that makes money forever without the requirement of your time, then you have a business that eventually results in massive freedom.

To really show the power of time detachment, I have a little story for you:

Once upon a time there was this quaint little village. It was a great place to live... except for one problem. The village had no water unless it rained. To solve this problem once and for all, the village elders asked contractors to submit bids to deliver water to the village on a daily basis. Two people volunteered to take on the task, and the elders awarded the contract to both of them.

The first person who won the contract, Ed, immediately ran out, bought two galvanized steel buckets and began running back and forth to the lake, which was a mile away. He immediately be-

gan making money as he labored morning to dusk, hauling water from the lake with his two buckets. He would empty them into the large concrete holding tank the village had built. Each morning he had to get up before the rest of the village awoke to make sure there was enough water for the people. It was hard work, but he was very happy to be making money and for having received one of the two exclusive contracts for this business.

The second winning contractor, Bob, disappeared for a while. He wasn't seen for months, which made Ed very happy, since he had no competition.

Instead of buying two buckets to compete with Ed, Bob wrote a business plan, found two investors, employed a president to do the work, and returned six months later with a construction crew. Within a year, his team had built a large-volume, stainless-steel pipeline which connected the village to the lake.

At the grand-opening celebration, Bob announced that he could supply the village with water 24 hours a day, 7 days a week. Ed could only deliver water on weekdays because he didn't want to work on weekends. Then Bob announced that he would charge 75% less than Ed did for this higher quality and more reliable water. The villagers cheered and immediately ran for the faucet at the end of Bob's pipeline.

In order to compete, Ed immediately lowered his rates by 75%, bought two more buckets, added covers to his buckets, and began hauling the four buckets each trip. In order to provide better service, he hired his two sons to give him a hand on the night shift and on weekends. When his boys went off to college, he said to them, 'Hurry back because someday this business will belong to you.'

Meanwhile, Bob realized that if this village needed water, then other villages must need water too. He rewrote his business plan and went off to sell his high-speed, high-volume, low-cost, clean-water delivery system to villages throughout the world.

He doesn't make a lot of money per bucket of water delivered, but he delivers billions of buckets of water every day. Whether he works or not, billions of people consume billions of buckets of water, and all that money pours into his bank account. Bob developed a pipeline to deliver money to himself, as well as water to the villages.

Bob lived happily ever after. Ed worked hard for the rest of his life and had never-ending financial problems. The end.

You see guys, Ed will never get wealthy and/or achieve freedom. Bob will forever make tons of money every single day while doing nothing. Ed is forever a slave. Bob is forever a wealthy legend. *Be like Bob.*

I first heard this story in Robert Kiyosaki's best-selling book *Rich Dad's Cashflow Quadrant.* In the book, he encourages readers to ask themselves, *Am I building a pipeline, or am I hauling buckets? Am I working hard, or am I working smart?*

I love this story because it perfectly highlights my point. It really shows how extremely crucial it is to create automatic systems instead of trading time for money. This is why some businesses owners can make billions of dollars while job workers make nothing. Because with a business that has this ingredient, it's a money-making system, a money machine. There are no limits.

But in a job, you're trading time for money. Since there's a limit on the amount of time we can give away and there's a limit on how much we can get paid per hour, there's a very low limit on how much money we can make with this method. **It is impossible to achieve wealth and freedom when we trade time for money.**

Unfortunately, there's a ton of 'business' owners who trade time for money. In my opinion, that's not a real business. That's a job in disguise. It's a boring, low-paying, enslaving, dysfunctional job that decided to dress up as a business for the costume party. There are so many businesses that only make money while the owner is working and it's a road heading straight to mediocrity or worse.

Let me just throw some examples at you really quick:

A private-practice chiropractor. He gets paid every time he works an hour. He's trading time for money and he will not achieve wealth and freedom.

A private-practice psychologist. He gets paid for every time he works with a patient. This is trading time for money and he will not achieve wealth and freedom.

So, chiropractors and psychologists can't get wealthy? Absolutely they can. Imagine if the chiropractor owned a clinic that functioned and made money without his presence. Imagine if he wrote a book about what he knew. These things would then be able to make him money without him working. He would've built a system, a money machine, and he would definitely have the opportunity to achieve wealth and freedom. Same thing with the psychologist.

The only way to achieve true financial freedom is to create, or buy, something that will make you money consistently without your presence. If your business requires you to work to make money, then it's a shitty business model that won't make you rich. To acquire the wealth and freedom you desire, you have to create some kind of system that can work, function and make money without you being there. This is a concept called *passive income* and it's the holy grail of financial freedom. I'll talk a lot more about that in part 3, though.

Jobs and private practices are cool IF...

It probably sounds like I hate jobs and job-like businesses. It probably even sounds like I'm suggesting that you can't get wealthy and free with a job. Well, that is in fact what I'm suggesting because it's the truth. UNLESS...

Unless you use that job or that private practice as a tool or as a stepping stone to creating a money-making system. If you're using your private practice to gather experience, money, clients, etc. to one day turn it into a real business. then it's a great idea.

Jobs and self-employment will not provide you wealth or freedom alone, but they can be used as stepping stones to something that will.

Whether you're working a job, you're self-employed, or you're running your own business, you should always work towards one day turning it into a money-making system. Because that is the only way to achieve the lifestyle you desire.

Here are some cool questions I suggest you ask yourself as soon as possible:

- Can my business be automated and systematized to operate while I'm absent?

- Are my margins thick enough to hire people to do the work?

- Will what I'm doing right now eventually lead to a money machine that doesn't require my time?

- Am I building a pipeline or am I hauling buckets?

- How can I get this business to operate exclusive of my time?

If there's anything I want you to take away from this subchapter, it's that if you're working hard on a business that isn't capable of ever functioning without your time and presence, you're wasting your time and money and you're setting yourself up for mediocrity. So, if you can't see any way that your business one day could turn into an automatic money machine, don't do it. It's a trap.

CONCLUSION

Control, scalability and time detachment: these are the three crucial ingredients. Without them, your business and your life as an entrepreneur will forever be mediocre. With these ingredients, there should be no limit on your potential and your opportunities to achieve.

A lot of entrepreneurs and business owners are not only mediocre but also slaves to their businesses. You now know how to avoid that. You know the three ingredients for huge, controllable, scalable, money systems that work for you while you're sleeping. With these ingredients, you'll have an incredible competitive advantage that will put you head and shoulders above everyone else.

CHAPTER BULLET POINTS:

- Many business owners are slaves to their businesses and they're mediocre because they didn't implement these three ingredients in their business models.

- Make sure you're fully in control over the important variables in business and in life.

- Scalability is a giant must if you want to do great things. If your way of making money isn't scalable at the moment, you should consider finding a way of implementing this ingredient. Play in the ocean, not the pool.

- The amount of money we make is a reflection of the amount of positive impact we have on people.

- Impact is the amount of people we help multiplied by the magnitude of our help. Don't limit your reach or magnitude.

- If you can't detach your time from your income, then you'll forever be a slave.

- Create a money machine. Build automatic systems that function without your presence, instead of trading your time away for money. Don't haul buckets, build pipelines.

[6]

CLARITY

Not many people have clarity. Actually, it's something that very few have. So many people are just walking around with no idea of what they really want in life. They have no idea where they want to go, and they certainly don't know how to get there.

Clarity is absolutely crucial and it's a must if you want to succeed in entrepreneurship and in life. With it, you will know where you want to go. Second, you'll know how to get there in the most effective way. We should all be crystal clear on our values, our visions, our goals, our dreams, etc. Clarity is a huge part of *The Cure for Mediocrity* because without it, we'll never escape mediocrity.

Without clarity, we'll get stuck. We'll be walking around in circles with no purpose or meaning. This is why you see some people at age 55 exactly where they were in their thirties. They have no idea where they're going, so they walk around in circles. No goals, no purpose, and no meaning.

Earlier in this book, we talked about knowing who we are, our skills, etc. We talked about self-awareness. When we're self-aware and we know who we are, our next step is to gain clarity.

Clarity is knowing where we want to go from where we are. Being self-aware is extremely important because we need to know who we are and where we are. Without clarity, though, we'll forever stay where we are.

Self-awareness is knowing who we are and where we are. Clarity is knowing who we want to be and where we want to go.

To move forward, we need to know which direction we want to go. Having true clarity is the only way to do that. We need to know our values and what makes us happy. We need to know our own definition of success. Also, a huge part of clarity is having dreams, visions and goals for the future. As you can imagine, these things are also crucial when it comes to success and achievement.

If we don't know where we're going, we'll end up somewhere else. If we don't have targets, we'll hit something else. If we're not on the road toward what we want, then we're on the road toward something we don't want. This means that if we're not crystal clear on what we want, we'll keep moving toward mediocrity. When we don't know our own definition of success, then we don't know which road leads there. When we don't know which road leads to success, we'll take a wrong road that will lead us to mediocrity.

So, without clarity, we'll either walk around in circles, going nowhere, or we will, even worse, move toward the opposite of our definition of success. This is why you can ask truly successful people questions like, *What are your goals for this month? Where do you want to be in a year?* and they'll tell you exactly where they want to be in every detail. If you ask a mediocre person these questions, he'll look at you strange.

Alright, so clarity is crucial as fuck and you need it if you want to succeed. *What does it mean, though?* Well, clarity is a wide concept. It's something we can have in a lot of different areas. Clarity is knowing, prioritizing and being clear. It's knowing what our values are. It's knowing where we want to go.

In this chapter, I'll be talking about the most crucial parts of clarity and how to get clear on those things. Hopefully, this chapter will make you crystal clear on your definition of success and then get you on the right path toward it.

VALUES

The first step to complete clarity is to be clear on your values. Before going any further toward our success journey, we have got to know what we value. We cannot have clarity and be clear on where we want to go without knowing what we value and what we don't. This means that getting clear on our values is something everyone should do as soon as possible.

Unfortunately, most people have no clue. I too didn't know what my values were. In fact, the first many times I heard about this concept, I ignored it because it sounded pretty stupid and also kind of intangible. What happens when we aren't clear on our values, though, is that what we attract into our lives becomes kind of random.

Instead of knowing exactly what we value and then focusing 100% on attracting that into our lives, we attract a little bit from here and a little bit from there. This means that a very small portion of what we're doing with our lives is actually making us happy, fulfilled, and moving us closer to our definition of success.

So, it is for this reason extremely crucial that we know our values. Also, we really have to be specific here. We can't just say,

Oh, I value happiness. That's not knowing your values. Knowing your values means that you know exactly what makes you happy and what doesn't. Being clear on our values means that we know red makes us frustrated while pink makes us excited.

It's also not enough to say, *I value love* because love can be expressed in tons of different ways. Saying you value love is not specific enough; it's not crystal clear. What we need to do instead is to find out what gives us the feeling of love.

Now, I don't wanna go all relationship expert on you right here because I'm really not. But there's a ton of different ways to get the feeling of love. Maybe you feel loved when you get a gift. Maybe you feel loved when someone spends time with you. Maybe a kiss is what gives you the feeling of love.

So, knowing your values is not as simple as saying, *I value love* or *I value happiness.* Knowing your values is when you know how to feel those feelings. Are you most happy when you're achieving, eating, watching TV, travelling, or being with your friends? Do you feel loved the most when someone gives you a gift or when someone tells you how much you mean to them? Are you the most confident when you're doing something you're good at or when you're looking at yourself in the mirror?

It's important to know our values and it's crucial that we're extremely specific. The reason we have to know our values is because we make all our decisions based on our values. **If we're not crystal clear on our values, our decisions will be random and we will attract random things into our lives.** If we have a pretty good idea about what our values are, we'll make some pretty good decisions that will attract some pretty good things into our lives. If we're crystal clear on our values, we'll focus 100% on what we value and, as a result, we'll attract only the best things into our lives.

This is when you turn into a world-class human being; When everything you attract into your life is exactly what you want. However, this can't happen without us being crystal clear on our values. All our decisions are based on what we value, so the clearer we can get on what we truly value in life, the better we can make the right decisions, which eventually will make us achieve our definition of success. **Our success is determined by our decisions and our decisions are determined by our values.**

> *"It's not hard to make decisions when you know what your values are." - Roy E. Disney*

I personally value excitement and adventure a lot more than I value security. To me, I'm happy when I'm trying to do big things. Trying to achieve what others might not think is possible gives me a ton of confidence. I also really value flexibility and freedom. I've always known that if I one day achieved the freedom to do whatever I wanted to, I'd be incredibly happy. Also, as cheesy as it might sound, I really enjoy helping others. Improving other people's lives gives me a sense of purpose. I value these things a lot more than security, safety, and certainty.

Because I know these things, I can easily make decisions that attract my values into my life. Since I like excitement more than safety, I'm more willing to pick the high-risk high-reward choice instead of the opposite. This also means that, contrary to what a lot of my friends and family want, I really want to travel the entire world and see everything, rather than staying in one place.

When picking my business model, I've decided to create something that eventually will provide freedom. I've decided to go all in on an idea with which I eventually can achieve the wealth and freedom I want. *Why?* Because I know I value freedom and flexibility. If I didn't know that, I wouldn't be able to make decisions congruent to that. If I wasn't able to do that when I first started out, I would be somewhere entirely different today. Know your values because you'll make your decisions based on what you value.

Something that's crucial to realize, however, is that not everyone has the same values. I wouldn't mind travelling non-stop for a year. My family members, however, would hate to be away from home for so long because they value the feeling of safety they have at home. This is a really important thing to realize. This means that you don't have to have the same values as your dad or your best friend.

It also means that you should be very careful about who you take advice from. What happens if someone who values freedom decides to listen to his English teacher for advice? What happens if someone who values security and safety decides to take advice from me? Well, what can sometimes happen is that the person giving the advice might give you advice based on his or her values instead of yours.

That's what I'm doing in this book. I'm giving advice based on my own values, not yours. This means that, if you really value security, you should probably be careful taking advice from me. What my advice will do is help you live a life full of flexibility, financial freedom and time to do what you love. Not getting a safe, secure job.

It can be very dangerous to take advice from people who don't share your values. What's even worse, though, is to take advice from someone who doesn't understand you. You see, even though my mother and I are completely different in every way possible, I can still take advice from her because she understands what I want. She understands my values and she gives me advice based on that knowledge.

So, if you want security, then you should take advice from someone who also values that or at least someone who understands it. If you want freedom, then I'm your guy because you and I are on the exact same path. You won't know who to take advice from if you don't know what you want, though.

So, the first step of complete clarity is to know our values. *What makes us happy? What makes us confident? What would make us feel fulfilled? What's our definition of success?*

I know some of this clarity and values shit might seem a little intangible. I remember how I felt about all of these things when I first heard about them. *What are you talking about? Just tell me which app to download and which stock I need to invest in, man.* I definitely don't blame you if you're feeling like these things are hard to take action on.

Trust me, though. Success, achievement, wealth, and all the other good stuff come from complete clarity. Complete clarity starts with knowing your values. If you're not crystal clear on your values, you'll get something else. Getting clear on these things is 100% worth it. I promise.

VISION

When you know what your values are, it's time to craft the ideal vision for your future. What would be your ideal lifestyle in five years? It's important to have a crystal clear vision for where you want to go and when you expect to be there. Having a vision is a huge part of clarity.

The way you craft a vision is by looking at your top values and then crafting a lifestyle out of that. Craft the perfect scenario. What's the best possible life you could have next year? In five years? In ten?

I have sold 100,000 copies of this book. I've helped millions of people around the world improve their lives and I get hundreds of emails every week from people saying I've changed their lives completely. I've built the #1 membership site for young people striving for the extraordinary lifestyle. And I've made millions in the process. The communities I've started are filled with thousands upon thousands of highly engaged people helping each other reach the next level in life and business. I'm speaking all over the world and I'm impacting a ton of people. Oh and yeah, I've also built a huge motivational clothing brand. I spend the majority of my profits on building a humongous real estate portfolio.

I'm gonna let you in on a little secret, though. *None of these things have happened yet.* This is where I want to be in a few years. This is *my vision.*

Having a vision like this makes it very easy for me to make decisions. I always know what I'm supposed to be doing. All I need to do is ask myself if what I'm doing at the moment will get me closer to my vision. If it doesn't, then I better have a good reason. If it does, then it motivates the crap out of me and I get incredibly inspired.

It shouldn't be that difficult to craft the perfect vision, to be honest. You can always change or adjust. I look at my vision and my goals every single day and I edit them nearly just as often.

Just imagine the ideal lifestyle you could be living next year or in 5 years.

When you have a mental picture of your ideal lifestyle, you have a vision and you'll have a lot more clarity. This will, like everything else in this book, put you head and shoulders above everyone else because very few people have a vision for the future.

VISUALIZATION

A very powerful thing to do, when we have a vision, is to visualize ourselves already being at the finish line. Visualize yourself already living the lifestyle you wish to someday live. *What does it look like? What does it feel like?* Take your vision, close your eyes, and then try your best to imagine it as vividly as possible.

When we visualize our desired future, our vision, we'll start believing that it's possible. It'll also motivate us like nothing else will. Let me ask you, when do you most want to eat a pizza? Is it when someone says the word "pizza" or when you're staring at the most delicious, fragrant pizza? Probably the last one, right? The same thing happens with our visions and our dreams. When we say the word "freedom," we get pretty motivated. When we can see, feel, touch, smell, and taste freedom, however, it's 400 times more motivating. It'll also make our vision seem more tangible, making it easier for us to take action.

Now, some of you might be thinking that this shit seems a little impractical, unreal, or even crazy. However, visualization is actually backed by science. This is not some self-help guru BS. This is legit, science-based practicality that we can all implement right away.

Here's what *The Huffington Post* has to say about visualization:

According to research using brain imagery, visualization works because neurons in our brains, those electrically excitable cells that transmit information, interpret imagery as equivalent to a real-life action. When we visualize an act, the brain generates an impulse that tells our neurons to "perform" the movement. This creates a new neural pathway — clusters of cells in our brain that work together to create memories or learned behaviors — that primes our bodies to act in a way consistent to what we imagined. All of this occurs without actually performing the physical activity, yet it achieves a similar result.

In other words, our brain cannot tell the difference between real experiences and something we've imagined very vividly. This means that we can imagine ourselves doing something and then, by doing that, we will create a neural pathway in our brain. This neural pathway will then remember the learned memory and/or behavior and we'll now know how to do it in reality. So, we can actually 'experience' something over and over just by imagining it vividly, thus making our brains and our bodies used to the thought of doing that specific activity.

I hope you realize how extremely powerful this is.

I use this all the time when I'm doing parkour. I'll visualize myself doing a specific move or jump. I'll do this over and over so that when I actually make the jump, I've already done it 15 times before. At least my brain and my body think so. And since I've already done it 15 times, my body is perfectly comfortable with the jump. What's there to be afraid of? I've already done it 15 times, *right?*

As we all know, if we've done something a lot of times, it becomes easy and it becomes natural. Remember when you were a kid and you were afraid of the big rollercoasters at the theme park? I remember I was. One thing all the rollercoasters had in common, though, was that if I had tried it once, I wouldn't be the least bit afraid of trying again.

You can get this feeling of confidence regarding your dreams and visions for your future. With visualization, you can experience all of your goals and visions before taking the first step toward them. This will eliminate, or at least decrease, your feelings of fear and doubt. It'll also make everything feel more comfortable and natural. Because you've already done it 15 times, *right?*

So, when you have a vision for your ideal future, the next step is to visualize and imagine it as vividly as possible. It'll change the entire game for you, I promise.

GOALS

"Setting goals is the first step in turning the invisible into the visible." - Tony Robbins

It might seem very hard to get started. It all feels so overwhelming. Remember the vision I was talking about earlier about where I want to be in a few years? To achieve a vision like that requires a ton of hard work. There are thousands of small things I need to do to achieve these things. *Where do I start? How long is it going to take? What should I prioritize? What's the first step toward my vision and my desired lifestyle?*

Well, setting goals will answer all of these questions. **With proper goal setting, you can look at where you want to be in 5 years and you'll know exactly what to do in this very moment.** You'll gain clarity, and all confusion will disappear. With the right goal setting, you'll know exactly what to do now to achieve your vision in the future. This is very powerful.

As with the other parts of clarity, goal setting is a part of not wandering around without purpose. With goals, you'll never walk in circles because you'll always be moving toward your goals. With goals, you'll always move forward and you'll always improve. Without goals, you'll walk around confused without getting anywhere. Imagine playing soccer without a goal. You'd be running around confused and you'd look stupid. Also, you'd never know when you actually scored. It's the exact same thing in life.

Another thing that goal setting will do for you is that it'll motivate the crap out of you. *Trust me.* I've lived without goals and I've lived with them. I get so much more done when I have goals because I'm 4803 times more motivated.

You see, without goals and deadlines, you'll procrastinate so much more. *Oh, I have to write those 1200 words for my book today. Well, no one will die if I skip today. The only thing that'll happen is that my book will be finished one day later. So what?* This way of thinking is extremely dangerous and it will kill momentum, it will kill productivity, and it will cause major procrastination.

When you have a goal to be finished with a specific project before a specific time, you will not allow yourself to procrastinate. You'll be so much more motivated and you won't procrastinate because you know that if you skip today, you'll fall short of your goal. You'll value your time a lot more, which is crucial.

Another thing that goal setting will do is that it'll give you a sense of urgency. I won't talk a lot about urgency right here because it'd take the rest of this book to really explain the importance and all the benefits. But urgency is when you feel like something has to be done as soon as possible. When something is urgent, you will not skip a day because finishing your project one day later would result in you not reaching your goal. **Procrastination stops when you have a sense of urgency. Urgency comes when you have a deadline.**

As you can see, goal setting has a lot of benefits and, for that reason, it's an extremely crucial thing to do. So, when you have your vision, your next step is to set goals congruent to that. Take small bits of what you want to achieve and turn them into goals.

Here are the questions I like to ask myself when setting goals for the future:

- Where do I want to be in 5 years?

- Where should I be in one year to achieve my 5 year goal?

- Where should I be in a month to achieve my one year goal?

- Where should I be in a week to achieve my one month goal?

- When I go to bed tonight, where should I be to achieve my one week goal?

- What do I have to get done within the next hour to achieve my one day goal?

- What should I do right now to achieve my one hour goal?

This way of setting goals will take an intangible, overwhelming future and turn it into something practical and simple that you can do right now. It is incredibly powerful. If you write these things down, you'll have an easier time remembering them and you'll also take everything more seriously. I always write my goals down.

So, when you have a picture of your perfect, ideal lifestyle, try this way of setting goals. It should give you complete clarity on what you need to do in order for you to achieve your goals.

TAKE ACTION

So, when you know what you're here to do, you know how you are going to build a business based on that, you know what your perfect vision is, and you've set goals congruently, your next step is to *take action*. Nothing in life comes without hard work and action.

> *"The key to success is to take massive, determined actions."*
> *- Tony Robbins*
>
> *"Action is the foundational key to all success." - Pablo Picasso*
>
> *"Take action to see reward. Do nothing and be ignored." - Matthew E. Fryer*
>
> *"You must take action now that will move you toward your goals. Develop a sense of urgency in life."- H. Jackson Brown, JR.*

Yeah, what these guys said. Sorry for the quote overload right there but I just really want you to realize that nothing in life will happen if you don't take *massive action*. Taking action toward your dreams is essential. Reading and educating yourself is extremely powerful and it will give you a competitive advantage that will put you head and shoulders above everyone who doesn't. Without action, however, none of what you read will help you. If you don't implement what you learn into your life, then reading is a waste of time. Remember, knowledge is not power. Knowledge is *potential* power.

I hope this chapter helped you gain a sense of clarity. I also hope that you'll take advantage of your clarity by taking action. I want the extraordinary lifestyle for you and, for that reason, I really hope you take the time to actually gain clarity. It's a long process and it takes commitment.

I'm sure a lot of people will read this chapter and continue their lives without implementing any of it. This won't improve your life, though. It's crucial that you commit to gaining complete clarity, setting congruent goals, and then taking action toward that. If you decide to do that, you'll very soon be on the road that leads to the world-class lifestyle you desire.

CHAPTER BULLET POINTS:

- Clarity is one of the most crucial parts of success and wealth. Without it, we'll be wandering around in circles with no purpose. This is what most people do.

- Most people aren't clear on their values. If we want the world-class lifestyle, however, we absolutely have to be clear. Our values determine our decisions and our decisions determine our outcomes and results.

- Being clear on our values is not simply saying, *I want to be happy.* Being clear on our values is knowing exactly what makes us happy and what doesn't.

- Craft the perfect vision for your ideal future. Make sure it's congruent with your values.

- Make it a daily habit to visualize you already living that vision.

- Set goals. Goal setting is a *huge key* for every great thing in life.

- Take massive, determined action.

PART 3:
CURING FINANCIAL
MEDIOCRITY

Why are some people extremely wealthy while others struggle to get by? What determines if one gets wealthy or not? We live in a world with 26-year-old billionaires and 65-year-old broke people. How is this possible? What ultimately causes these differences? What are the determinants?

Is it because a select few were chosen by the universe to become wealthy? Is it because they have rich parents? Is it because of where they live? Is it luck? Is it because they work harder than normal people?

Well, actually, it's *none* of those things. Hard work is without a doubt necessary to achieve success and wealth. However, I know a lot of people who work extremely hard and are still not swimming in cash. What about the miners in Africa? They certainly work hard, day in day out, but I wouldn't call them extremely wealthy. Hard work is definitely not the differentiator between poor, middle-class, and wealthy people.

[7]

WEALTH GAME PLAN 1 & 2

The main determinant of your financial future is the wealth game plan you decide to follow. The road you decide to travel. You see, different game plans have different outcomes. Different roads have different destinations.

So, it doesn't matter how hard you work if you're on a road that is going the opposite direction of your desired destination.

Imagine this. I show you a 1000-mile road that leads to a dead end. I convince you to travel this road, even though it doesn't lead to anything you want. You can crawl, walk, run, bike or even take your car to get to the end. But it won't matter how fast you're going; you'll never reach your desired destination if the road you're on doesn't lead to your dreams.

This is the problem for a lot of people. Actually, it's the problem for about 97% of people. They're on a shitty road leading to a place they don't want to be. Then, when they don't reach their desired destination, they blame themselves for not working hard enough or they blame their circumstances. They keep working and they keep hoping. It's a cycle that leads to dead ends and misery.

Unfortunately, these people will never reach their desired destinations. They'll end up somewhere completely different and they don't even know why. **Working extremely hard on the wrong path will not take you where you want to go. You'll just arrive at your undesired destination faster.**

I like to visualize my wealth game plan as my road and my work ethic as my vehicle. The faster the vehicle I have, the faster I'll get to the destination of my road. That doesn't matter if I'm on a shitty road, though. I'd rather walk on the right path than drive a fast car on the wrong one. Work ethic is crucial but without the proper game plan, you'll never become wealthy.

The game plan you follow will determine your perspective and beliefs around money. Your perspective and beliefs will determine your decisions and actions. Your decisions and actions will determine your results and outcomes. So, as you can see, the first step toward wealth is to start following the right game plan. Your actions will then be based on the right game plan and you'll be on your journey toward your desired destination.

With the wrong game plan, it can be almost impossible to achieve your desired results. Unfortunately, we live in a society where we only hear about one game plan. People like us, who want more out of life, are unsure of what to do because no one told us how to be great. We haven't been informed about the game plan we need to achieve our desired outcomes.

The thing is, not a lot of people are willing to say the things you'll read about in this chapter. Not a lot of people have the balls to actually tell you the truth. *Why?* Because it's tough being controversial. It's tough telling people that what they've always been told isn't really the best way of doing things. However, I strongly feel that everyone is entitled to at least knowing about the different game plans. It's not fair that we're only told about one of them.

After the next two chapters, however, you should know more about the three different game plans and their usual outcomes. I'll try my best to make sure that you don't leave these chapters without knowing what you need to know to make a decision. A decision about which road you choose to take. Which game plan you decide to follow.

Now, I certainly won't tell you which one to choose. I'd never do that. Because, you see, everyone has different preferences, priorities, and dreams for the future. It would be wrong of me to tell you which one you should pick. I can, however, make a recommendation. I'd pick the last one at all times. I think you'll enjoy the last option as well. Pick the last option, man. You should definitely pick game plan number three. It's up to you, though (pick the last one).

Let's get into the first one.

1. The Game Plan of Poverty

The first game plan is one you probably don't want to choose. By taking this road, you'll be heading straight toward poverty, bankruptcy, and misery. The people on this road will always be one-something-from-broke. One *layoff* from broke. One *injury* from broke. The list goes on. With this game plan, you'll always be incredibly fragile because if anything changes in your life, you'll be homeless.

What's the destination for this game plan? Well, there isn't one. With this game plan, you couldn't care less about tomorrow as long as you're having fun right now. People living this way have a motto that says: "fuck tomorrow because I might not be here tomorrow." They sacrifice tomorrow for a pleasurable to-day.

"Oh yeah, that's what I'm talking about, let's go! I just found $27 in my pocket! Let's quickly buy something stupid because, you know, you can't take money with you when you die." Or "Woohoo! I made $200 more this month than I did last month. This means I can party even harder this weekend."

People who follow this game plan will always spend whatever they have *right now*. They'll always spend all of their money on materialistic things and they'll spend their time on pure "fun" and stupidity. If they make $4200 a month, guess how much they're spending every month? If you said $4200, you wouldn't be totally wrong. However, they actually spend *more*. They spend whatever they make, plus a little extra on the credit card. These are the people who take all kinds of loans to get the newest things, just to put themselves into greater debt. *For what?* To "enjoy today," of course! This way of thinking usually ends in bankruptcy.

People following the game plan of poverty will create a life-style in direct proportion to their income. These people will then supplement that lifestyle by use of bad debt.

With the constant "sacrifice tomorrow for a pleasurable to-day" mentality, these folks will never arrive at any destination. They'll just keep doing the same things over and over. Unfortu-nately, though, you can't keep buying things on credit and pay-ment plans. Eventually, this way of living will become completely miserable. They'll still live for today and shit all over their future, but it'll only get harder and harder to sustain that kind of life-style.

This road could also be called, "The game plan of complete instant gratification" because it revolves around immediate pleasure instead of long term pleasure. This will result in long term pain.

These people will most likely never get wealthy because wealth is a long process of creating and building. **If you never build, you'll never have an empire.** Unfortunately, for people with this game plan, it's not about being wealthy, it's about *appearing* wealthy. It's not about having a ton of money, it's about having a ton of materialistic things (that put you in debt) to make you look like you have *tons* of money.

Besides, one day they'll "hit it big" so why would they spend time building something now? People on this game plan believe wealth is an event. It's something that just happens if you do the right thing once. Many of these people also believe that success and wealth is about luck. If the universe wants them to be wealthy, it'll come to them somehow. By the way, these are also the people who buy lottery tickets - not for fun, but because they actually believe that's their opportunity to wealth.

To give you a better idea about the people on this game plan, let me show you some of the usual viewpoints of people who follow this road:

- *If I want it now, I'll get it now. I can pay for it some other day.*

- *I don't value my time at all. I don't mind flushing all my time down the toilet by watching TV or spending 4 hours on social media. Also, I'd gladly spend 2 hours of my time to make $7. Money is valuable while time is not, right?*

- *When I have money, I spend it. You only live once, right?*

- *Yay! I'm finally finished with school! I never have to read a book again in my life. I can stop educating myself now.*

- *My purpose? Skills? Passions? Man, I'm just taking whatever job pays the most.*

- *My plans for the future? Heck, I don't even know if I'm gonna be here tomorrow. Why would I spend my time, energy, and resources on the future?*

- *The reason I'm not wealthy is because I'm unlucky, my boss sucks, my parents suck, I've had a tough upbringing, it's not possible for me, and blablabla.*

- *I've done whatever I can to become successful in life. It's not my fault I've been dealt a shitty hand. I'd love to see the successful people go through what I've gone through.*

- *Insurance? People keep telling me how important it is to have it. I just don't feel like it's a priority. Besides, I'm never gonna benefit from it because nothing will happen to me.*

Now, I hope you don't get offended if some of these examples reflect your beliefs, opinions, and perspectives. Trust me, I've had some of these thoughts and viewpoints during my life. However, I want you to realize that these beliefs will pull you closer and closer toward poverty and misery.

Another crucial thing to realize is that this game plan is followed by every income bracket. The amount of money you make does not determine which game plan you follow. Everyone, from the homeless to the people making millions, can find themselves on this very road. You can follow the game plan of wealth (game plan 3) if you have a low income; conversely, someone who's making millions can still be on this road and end up bankrupt, poor, and financially stressed.

Here are two awesome quotes from MJ DeMarco's book, *The Millionaire Fastlane*:

> *"Financial discipline is blind to income."*

> *"More money is not a solution to poor financial management."*

I love these quotes by MJ because they eliminate the belief that higher income means more wealth. **More money doesn't fix a lack of financial literacy.** Sometimes, a higher income can mean even more poverty. You could make millions but if you burn all of it, you won't get any richer.

Remember when I said that people on this game plan design their lifestyles around the amount of money they make, plus an extensive use of debt? Well, if someone who makes $4200 a month decides to spend $4500 a month, is that person richer or poorer than the one who makes $42000 and spends $45000? The last guy is not better off because he, too, doesn't get wealthier at all but he puts himself in more debt.

More money usually means more expenses too. The guy with more money has a bigger house and two big cars instead of one small one. If you spend your entire income on buying expenses, then more money is *not* a good thing. It will actually make you poorer as you'll find yourself in greater debt. I'm gonna talk a lot more about assets and liabilities later, though.

This instant gratification game plan is a lot of fun in the short term. However, as you've probably also noticed, the future for people on this game plan does not look appealing. With this

"Screw tomorrow. YOLO!" mindset, you'll end up in a ton of trouble. I get that this lifestyle might be fun, but be careful when making the decision to live this way because, if you keep living this way, you'll eventually find yourself in a great deal of shit. You'll be drowning in debt.

Now, I'm not saying that you shouldn't enjoy the present. The problem with the next game plan is that it doesn't allow you to enjoy today at all. And I'm a huge fan of enjoying today. I just don't feel that sacrificing tomorrow is the right way to do it. I do everything I can to get the best out of every single day while still setting myself up for a great tomorrow. So enjoy today, but care about your future.

2. THE GAME PLAN OF MEDIOCRITY

Ah, the game plan of mediocrity. The game plan followed by the vast majority. This is the way your mom, your biology teacher, and your friend, John, view wealth and life.

Most people follow this game plan because we've been force-fed these ideas since we were children. Society keeps telling us that this game plan is the best way to achieve wealth and that you'll reach freedom, prosperity, and joy at the end of this road. The system, without even asking us what we *want*, puts everyone on this game plan. From the age of 5 or 6, we get indoctrinated, brainwashed, and even programmed, to this way of living. The thing that's messed up here isn't that the game plan sucks. It's that it's the only game plan they show us and prepare us for.

One of the most characterizing things about this game plan is the 5:2 ratio. Working hard for 5 days to get a 2-day weekend. A lot of people on this game plan live for Friday night. They work at a boring job for 5 days and then, finally, it's Friday. "Yay, I can now enjoy my life for two days - I better make the most of it!" If your Saturday is better than your Tuesday, then you're currently on this game plan.

I've brought a once-in-a-lifetime opportunity for you here today. You give me $5k and then, in return, I'll give you $2k. How does that sound? Pretty appealing, huh? Well then, let's do this every week for the rest of your life. Sound good? In my opinion, it sounds like a ridiculous, losing strategy.

Now, if you *love* your job, then this is obviously not the case for you. Make sure you're maximizing that opportunity. I'm talking about the people feeling miserable 5 days a week because they're doing something they hate. The people who only truly live when it's the weekend. The ones trading 5 days of happiness to get 2 in return. You'd be surprised how big a percentage of people actually live this way.

TIME FOR MONEY: THE *WORST* TRADE YOU CAN MAKE.

Another very characterizing feature of the game plan of mediocrity is the trade-off between time and money. Trading an hour of your time to get paid a small amount of money. Working seemingly endless hours every week to get paid by someone else. You give him your time, he'll pay you a little bit of money in return.

The problem with this way of generating income is that it relies on your *time*. Remember when we talked about time detachment? I was serious when I said it's the most important ingredient for freedom. If you trade your time for money, you'll only get paid when you spend your time. If you spend your time on something else, you get nothing.

The dangerous thing about this is that, when you grow more and more successful, you'll have less and less time and freedom.

The more successful you become at trading time for money, the less time you'll have. This is why you see incredibly successful lawyers, doctors, managers, engineers, etc. (all time-for-money traders) work 70-85 hours a week without time for their children, fun, or relaxing. The better they become, the more work they get to do.

> *"By working faithfully 8 hours a day, you may eventually get to be the boss and work 12 hours a day." - Robert Frost*

Trading time for money is what almost everyone does these days, including tons of "business owners" and entrepreneurs. When we work, we get paid. When we don't work, we don't get paid. As you can imagine, when your way of creating income is to give away your time, it's actually impossible to have much of both. You can either have a lot of time but no money or you can have a lot of money but no time.

THE PURSUIT OF HAPPINESS

So, why do we sacrifice money, time, freedom, etc. to get an education and a job? Why do we sacrifice fun experiences? Why don't we, on a Tuesday, enjoy the nice weather, spend time with friends and family, party, travel, etc? Why do we decide to work instead of doing these fun things?

Well, we do all these things to receive money, freedom, and safety. If we get money, freedom and safety, then we can do fun things. We sacrifice the things that make us happy so that we can get a job. We work that job to make money. The reason we want money is because we want to be happy.

We all want to be happy. We also know what it is that makes us happy. We don't do these things, though. *Why?* Because we're too busy. Too busy *doing what?* We're too busy getting a degree, working at a job, and saving for retirement. Why do we do these things? Because we think it'll make us *happy.*

In 2007, The Washington Post performed an experiment that helps to prove my point:

He arrived at the L'enfant Plaza and positioned himself against a wall beside a trash basket. He was just a young white man in jeans, a long-sleeved T-shirt and a baseball cap. From a small case, he grabbed a violin. He put a few dollars in his small case and put it at his feet so people could donate.

It was 8am, on Friday, the middle of the morning rush hour. In the next 43 minutes, as the violinist played six classical pieces, 1,097 people passed by. Almost all of them were in a rush because they were on their way to their corporate jobs.

Each passerby had a quick decision to make. Do you stop and listen? Do you hurry past with a blend of irritation? Do you throw in a buck just to be polite? Does your decision change if he's really bad? What if he's really good? Do you have time for beauty? Shouldn't you?

Three minutes went by before something happened. Sixty-three people had already passed when, finally, there was a breakthrough of sorts. A middle-aged man looked at the violinist for a split second, turning his head to notice that there seemed to be some guy playing music. Yes, the man kept walking, but it was something. A half-minute later, the violinist got his first donation. A woman threw in a buck and scooted off. It was not until six minutes into the performance that someone actually stood against a wall and listened. However, there was never any kinds of crowd.

Things never got much better. In the three-quarters of an hour that the violinist played, seven people stopped what they were doing to hang around and take in the performance, at least for a minute. Twenty-seven gave money, most of them on the run -- for a total of $32 and change. That leaves the 1,070 people who hurried by, oblivious, many only three feet away, few even turning to look.

No one knew it but the fiddler standing against a bare wall outside the Metro was one of the finest classical musicians in the world, playing some of the most elegant music ever written on one of the most valuable violins (that's a $3.5 million price tag) ever made.

The musician was Joshua Bell, an internationally acclaimed virtuoso and one of the greatest, most celebrated violinists of his era. Three days before he appeared at the Metro station, Bell had filled the house at Boston's stately Symphony Hall, where merely pretty good seats went for $100. Two weeks later, at the Music Center at Strathmore, in North Bethesda, he would play to a standing-room-only audience so respectful of his artistry that they stifled their coughs until the silence between movements. But on that Friday in January, Joshua Bell was just another mendicant, competing for the attention of busy people on their way to work.

Bell decided to begin with "Chaconne" from Johann Sebastian Bach's Partita No. 2 in D Minor. Bell calls it "not just one of the greatest pieces of music ever written, but one of the greatest achievements of any man in history." It's a spiritually powerful piece, emotionally powerful, and structurally perfect. The piece is said to be a celebration of the breadth of human possibility.

Yet almost no one paid attention.

So, one of the greatest violinists in the world is playing one of the greatest, most beautiful pieces of music in history on a violin worth $3.5 million, yet no one is paying attention? No one had time to stop and enjoy this beautiful experience. When this guy is playing his music, it usually costs hundreds of dollars to experience. When we get it for free on our way to work, however, we don't even want it?

People had an opportunity to experience something great and beautiful, but they didn't. *Why?* Because they were on their way to work. Why do they work? To do something fun during the weekends - e.g. going to a concert.

This story perfectly demonstrates how people on this game plan are sacrificing things that make them happy. Why? Because they want to happy. This is so ironic. People on this game plan are literally sacrificing happiness in the pursuit of happiness. Unfortunately, in this trade, we get less back than we give. It's, for this reason, a very dangerous trade to continuously be making.

WEALTH AND MONEY

So far, I've been talking about how people on the game plan of mediocrity view life. Now, let's talk about how they view wealth and money.

First, let's look at their way of generating income. With the game plan of mediocrity, we generate all our income by trading our time away. We give an hour of our time to receive a paycheck in return. For every hour we work, we get paid. The amount we make per hour is determined by our salary, which is often determined by our work ethic and the value of our skills.

Second, with the game plan of mediocrity, our way of creating wealth is to save. Every time we get paid, we put a little chunk of it aside and save it for the future. Then, with a few percentages of interest, we hope that compound interest will make us wealthy when we're 65.

Third, to speed up and improve the process, people on this game plan rely on pay raises if they want to get wealthier faster. A pay raise can happen if we work harder, work more hours, get an additional degree, or go through certain training programs. By getting a 3% pay raise, we can speed up the journey to wealth because now we can contribute even more to our savings. So the way to get wealthier, on this game plan, is through more education and harder work.

Unfortunately, the likelihood of becoming truly wealthy this way is really, really small - almost *non-existent*. Let me ask you: how many people do you know who live this way? How many of them have an abundance of money and can do whatever they want to? Probably not many.

Now, there are definitely many people who make a killing trading time for money. I know people who I believe will become wealthy, even though they're generating wealth this way. However, compared to all the people who'll never become wealthy, it's not amazing odds. This way of creating wealth is definitely one road to wealth. However, I don't believe it's the optimal way. I have this belief because I've seen so many people work 75 hours a week on a great job and still aren't anywhere near becoming wealthy and financially free.

A job can make you very wealthy, but not on its own. More on this later, though.

MATH

So, why is this *not* the best way to get wealthy? Why is it that so many people on this game plan will never be wealthy and free?

Well, math.

I'm not just coming up with suggestions based on opinions, I'm coming with suggestions based on facts and math - especially when it comes to money and numbers. You see, the game plan of mediocrity does not have math on its side. There are so many numbers involved in wealth and, to be honest, this mediocre, middle-class way of thinking is just conflicting with the numbers that you need. **Math makes it very difficult for wealth to be created by trading time for money.**

What am I talking about? Well, I'm talking about all the variables. *Think about it.* To get wealthy this way, you have to depend on a lot of variables, like your hourly wage, hours worked, interest on your savings, etc. There are so many variables included in a wealth game plan and, unfortunately, the variables in this game plan all have limits.

Check this out:

- **Wages:** The limit on this is determined by so many things. However, there's almost always a limit on how much you can get paid for your time.

- **Hours:** Your limit here is 24 hours a day. Realistically, your limit is about 16-18 hours of work per day. Ultimately, you will never be able to work more than 24 hours in a day.

- **Interest on savings:** There'll always be a limit on the interest your bank will pay you to keep your savings with them.

- **Expenses:** You cannot survive with $3 a month. When it comes to expenses, we all have a limit on how little we can spend.

- **Years you live:** The more years you live, the more you can work and contribute to your savings. However, you're not gonna be 231 years old. There's a limit on the amount of years you can live.

These are just a couple of examples. There are a lot more variables involved in creating wealth. On this game plan, almost all of them are limited.

These are the most crucial and most determining variables when it comes to creating wealth and, with this game plan, they're all extremely limited. Math is working against this game plan.

Yes, you can work more, but there's only so many hours in a day. Yes, you might be able to increase your savings' interest rates by 0.5%, but there's a ceiling. Yes, you can live below your means, but you have to survive. Yes, you can increase the amount of years you live by eating healthy and exercising, but again there's a limit.

They all have *limits.*

GURUS

When people start to realize that their game plan isn't working - it isn't making them wealthy, at all - they start going to gurus and financial experts for help. When these gurus aren't busy talking about some random stock that really doesn't matter, they'll tell you to avoid all debt and to keep contributing to your 401(k). The second you turn off the show, they're laughing while wiping their asses with money because, trust me, they make a lot of money by giving you bullshit advice like that.

They'll tell you to quit drinking Starbucks because, hey, if you don't drink a $5 coffee every Sunday, you'll have $20 more every month. "Also, put more air in your tires because you'll save money on gas. I know it doesn't sound like much, but saving 5 cents every week can, and will, make you a millionaire when you're old. The secret to wealth? Don't spend anything that isn't required for you to survive."

"Each cent you apply toward diminishing your debt replenishes you."

I really don't mean to be rude but... BWAHAHAHAHAHA... Sorry.

Now, I'm not saying these financial experts you see on the news are all scamming you just to make a lot of money themselves... *But they are.* After you see them on the news, you buy their books, which again just tells you to live below your means, and then they get famous and can sell even more bullshit. They'll give you these stupid examples of how, if you saved $1000 in 1970, you would be a millionaire now.

Now, they're definitely not lying to you. They're just not telling you more than 3% of the entire truth. When they tell you shit like, "if you had invested $1000 back in 1965, you'd have $1 million today," they don't tell you about interest, inflation, or risk. They don't tell you that you'd have to have a steady 15% interest rate every single year for 50 years in a row for that to have happened. They don't tell you that, back then, $1000 was worth around $7700 today. They don't tell you about the risks. If the market crashes, there goes 30% of your savings which might have taken you 10 years to accumulate.

By the way, saving is an amazing thing to do and I encourage everyone to do it. However, saving should not be a way of *creating* wealth. You should not be saving just to save. You see, I save money too. But I don't do it just to save. I do it to invest. If you're saving money to invest in assets or in business, then it's an amazing thing to do. I'm gonna be talking a lot more about these things later, though.

Anyway, back to those financial gurus I don't like. Now, there are some extremely great financial experts out there who you can learn a lot from. However, most of them, especially the ones you see on TV, are scamming you and they're making a ton of money in the process.

How do you think these financial advisors became worth millions? By investing 10% of their $37k salary for 15 years? Or by writing 7 bestsellers and selling them over and over again to innocent people?

Listen, I don't mind that these people are making huge bank by writing books. What I do mind, however, is that they lie about how they got rich. They're actually telling you that you should work hard in a safe, secure job and save. Meanwhile, they haven't had a job in 15 years because they're creating programs, courses, and writing books on how to have a job and save. They're telling you to do A, while they're getting rich by doing B.

So, I dislike these people who talk about how to get rich. What about me, then? Isn't that what I'm doing myself? Yes, indeed it is. HOWEVER, there's a huge distinction here that you must realize. I'm actually practicing what I preach.

You see, these people are telling you to work hard at a safe job while they're out there creating businesses. I'm telling you to create something valuable that can impact other people in a positive way - this way, you'll have a profitable business. What am I doing? I'm creating something valuable that can impact other people in a positive way - this way, I'll have a profitable business.

Disclaimer: This book has the potential to make me money. But the reason this book is not a scam is because I'm completely honest about it and, more importantly, I'm practicing what I preach. So, instead of telling you to do something stupid that'll never make you money, I'm gonna tell you how to actually get wealthy. And yes, I might make money in the process, which just proves my point that creating something of value is the way to go. I'm telling you to do B while I'm doing B!

Here are some key distinctions between me and most financial "gurus":

- They make a lot more money than I do because it's easier to sell people on what they already believe than it is to sell the truth. Selling controversy is very challenging compared to what they're doing.

- They're telling you to get rich by doing A (which doesn't work) while they're getting wealthy by doing B.

- They're dishonest and they don't care about you. They care about their bank accounts more than meaningful impact. I'm the opposite.

- 95% of people love them while only a select few will listen and implement what I have to say. Why? Because I'm controversial and I'm telling the truth. I'm not gonna tell you what you want to hear, I'm gonna tell you what you need to hear. This way, you'll actually get results.

I'm not telling you to hate every financial "guru" in the world. I'm just telling you to get a little suspicious when you hear someone preach that the way to get wealthy is through buying less Starbucks coffee. Especially if they're telling you that they got rich that way.

A GAMBLE OF HOPE

Now, with this game plan, there are a lot of things that you can control. However, there are even more that you can't. That's why I call the game plan of mediocrity a gamble of hope. There are so many things that have to happen for you to succeed with this game plan. Many of which you can't control.

Hope is not a plan.

The reason that this game plan is a plan of hope is because there are so many variables included. There are so many things that you just *hope* are gonna happen because you can't control them.

Here's some of the variables included in this game plan:

- You having a job
- How hard, and how much, you work
- The housing market
- The stock market
- Your interests
- Inflation
- Your expenses

So, how many of these variables are important? How many of these could single-handedly ruin you, or make you wealthy? All of them. How many of them do you control? Two of them. Don't tell me that's a safe and secure game plan, much less a road to wealth.

You can't control the market. You can't control your interests, inflation, or even you having a job. You might be highly educated but if there's not a current need for your skills, you'll be fucked.

The only thing you can control is how hard you work, in case you have a job. And then, of course, your expenses. You can control how much you spend.

This means that you can work extremely hard while spending nothing, doing everything you can to achieve wealth, and still never achieve it. There are just way too many things that you can't control compared to how many you can. The consequence of this is that everyone on this game plan is working as hard as possible, spending as little as possible, and then crossing their fingers, wishing that all the uncontrollable, third-party variables don't fuck everything up.

The game plan of mediocrity is a plan of hope. A plan of hope is not a real plan.

To top it off, all the variables are limited. Like I talked about earlier in this chapter, all of these variables are limited and they're not scalable. There's a limit on how hard you can work, how good the markets can be, your interests, your expenses, etc. So, not only is this game plan based on hope, it's also not scalable. This means that even *best case scenario*, if you're lucky, isn't wealth. It's like playing a game where you can either lose, or you can lose even more.

I hope this chapter didn't offend you. There's absolutely nothing wrong with being on either of these game plans. As I said earlier, I have a lot of friends and family members on these game plans and I love them to death. I just want you to have clear expectations. It's cool to follow these game plans, but don't expect the wealth and freedom everyone is promising you.

Here are some typical viewpoints from people on the game plan of mediocrity:

- *I make money when I trade my time away.*

- *I have an abundance of time and I'm never gonna grow old or die.*

- *All debt is bad and I must avoid it like the plague.*

- *Schooling is important because it leads to better jobs.*

- *If I want to be a multimillionaire, I have to save every cent I don't need.*

- *I have one source of income - my job.*

- *Compound interest will turn my $37 into $40 million if I give it enough time.*

- *The dream is to be able to have a decent retirement when I'm 65.*

- *I don't wanna take risks, and I ignore my dreams. I want safety and security.*

- *My home is an asset.*

- *I'm living below my means for 40 years because I want to eventually have freedom.*

- *If someone got wealthy without staying in school until they were 30, then that's pure luck and they're 1 out of a million. This should not be encouraged.*

- *My biggest chance of increasing my income is to get a promotion.*

- *I sacrifice happiness in the pursuit of happiness.*

- *My Saturdays are better than my Tuesdays.*

Again, there's nothing wrong with these viewpoints. I'm sure you agreed with some of them. I did for a long time. Almost everyone I know has these viewpoints. So, please don't feel discouraged. At least you now know which beliefs might be holding you back from achieving massive success and wealth.

P.S. Don't ever force these game plans on people who desire wealth and freedom. I see a lot of mediocre parents force these game plans on their children. I see a lot of mediocre friends forcing these game plans on their ambitious friends. If someone suggests one of these game plans because he/she doesn't know better, simply educate them on what you're learning in these chapters. If they force these game plans on you to pull you down, cut the relationship immediately. You don't need them in your life.

CHAPTER BULLET POINTS:

- Hard work is a necessity, not the key for success. Working hard doesn't matter if you're not working right. Remember the pipeline vs buckets story.

- A big income will never solve money problems if your problem is illiteracy.

- The game plan of mediocrity, the one society automatically puts us on, is about trading our time away for money and relying on one source of income - a job.

- When one becomes successful at trading his time away for money, he'll be rewarded with even more work hours. Work 8 hours to eventually get promoted and work 12 hours. When our way of making money is to trade our time away, it'll be impossible to have a lot of both.

- On the game plan of mediocrity, people often sacrifice happiness in the pursuit of happiness.

- Math and numbers make the game plan of mediocrity uncontrollable and unscalable. With this game plan, it's incredibly difficult to become truly wealthy. There are so many variables in this game plan that conflict with math.

- Most financial "gurus" are getting rich by doing the exact opposite of what they're telling you to do.

- The game plan of mediocrity is built around hope, luck, and tailwind. Hope is not a plan.

- There's nothing wrong with being on either of these game plans. However, you should have clear expectations. Don't expect to get wealthy by following these game plans, like society is promising you.

[8]

WEALTH GAME PLAN 3

So, we've talked about the game plan of poverty - the plan for those screwing their futures for a better today. The people who live only in the present and who don't give a damn about tomorrow. These people usually enjoy life while they're young. Their future, however, is often not very glamourous because they're deep in debt. They've gotten so caught up in enjoying life that they didn't bother building a future for themselves.

We've also talked about the game plan of mediocrity - the middle-class game plan. On this plan, people sacrifice today in hopes of a better tomorrow. They don't allow any joy into their daily lives because they're too busy chasing a future joy. These people usually enjoy life when they're older. Mostly in their fifties, sixties, and seventies - because that's when their persistence finally pays off.

Their youth, however, is usually sacrificed and spent on school, education, and hard work in corporate jobs. They've gotten so caught up in building a future for themselves that they don't enjoy their youth. People on this game plan usually don't enjoy this beautiful journey of life because they're busy trying to reach a destination they believe will make them happy.

We haven't talked about the last game plan, though. This is very normal because no one is talking about this game plan except the ones who are living it. Our society doesn't tell us anything about this game plan. The system doesn't give us a chance to pick this game plan. Our parents shit their pants even thinking about their kids choosing this way of living. Altogether, we're not really getting a proper chance to take a shot at this game plan.

This obviously results in very low percentages of people deciding to do it. When no one is telling us about it, much less teaching us *how* to do it, it can be very difficult and challenging to pursue this mysterious, unknown road to wealth. This is why I'd like to bet $17 that everyone you know is living on one of the two roads I talked about in the last chapter. *Am I right?* Personally, until I started reaching out and purposely networking with people on this game plan, I didn't know anyone who did it either.

And, even when we know that we want to follow this game plan, it can be difficult to find the proper guidance. It can be challenging to find proper information on how to actually do it. Guidance regarding this game plan is rare because of the low amount of people using it. Especially good guidance that isn't trying to scam you. **Information is at an all-time high while proper guidance is at an all-time low.**

So, most people decide that it's too overwhelming to get into. Even the ones who actually find proper guidance regarding this game plan might hesitate because of fear. It's scary doing the opposite of what everyone else is doing. It's especially terrifying if you think about failing in front of your family and friends. It's very scary to tell everyone else that you're gonna do the opposite of what they are doing. Fear of failure, and embarrassment, hold a lot of people back.

So, that's three reasons for why people aren't using this game plan:

1. Most people don't know about it.

2. The ones who do know about it don't know how to do it.

3. The ones do who know how to do it hesitate and procrastinate due to a fear of failure.

So, there are really three layers, or barriers, that you have to go through before you pursue this game plan. And, since society and the system don't help us through any of them, a lot of people think it's too overwhelming and they decide to follow one of the other two game plans. They settle.

So, who are the select few who follow this game plan?

Well, not many people get through all three barriers. The select few who do are the ones we all admire. The ones who want more out of life. The ones who strive to become the best they possibly can. The ones who realize that life is a one-time thing and we won't get a second chance. People on this game plan are the ones hungry enough to go for crazy dreams that are 200 times bigger than the average person's dreams. The ones who want to maximize this ONE shot we have at life.

"Stop acting like you live twice." - Gary Vaynerchuk

People on this game plan have a sense of urgency. They don't procrastinate, and they certainly don't tell themselves lies like "one day I'll do it. It doesn't have to be now, though." You know,

I'm very young. Yet, when I look at a world map, I feel like I'm in a rush because I want to see everything in every country. I feel a sense of urgency because I realize that if I want to achieve a tenth of what I want in life, I better start now.

I have tons of dreams and ideas. The problem is I only expect to live about 100 years.

This is the way people on this game plan think. They want to see, have, be, give, feel, and experience so much that they just refuse to procrastinate. They refuse to sacrifice everything just to have fun at age 65. They want everything life has to offer and they're not afraid to reach for it.

So, *where do these people end up?* Well, these people have the courage and the hunger to pursue their purposes and their dreams. So, *that's* where they end up. They end up living the amazing lifestyles that most only dream about. They end up having complete financial freedom because they decided to get it. They end up in great shape because they decided to do it. They end up traveling the world and experiencing life in a different way. *Why?* Because they realized they wanted to, and then they did it.

This game plan is for people who value freedom, excitement, adventure, and fun a lot more than security, safety, and comfort. This game plan is for the courageous people who dare to chase their dreams regardless of how many people are telling them not to. It's for people who wanna do the opposite of what everyone else is doing to eventually live the life they desire.

So, is this game plan for you? Well, if you desire wealth, freedom, and fun, then this is your game plan. If you're afraid of doing the opposite of others and you value security and safety, then I'd recommend the second game plan, which is great, too.

FREEDOM

One of the many reasons to follow this game plan is the freedom it can provide. By doing it right, this game plan will provide complete freedom - financially and timewise. This is very attractive for many. In my opinion, this game plan is the only way to truly achieve that at a young age.

Remember the story about the village in need of water? One guy kept running back and forth between the river and the village. This guy would never achieve freedom. He would continue doing that all his life without ever increasing in freedom or wealth. The other guy, however, built a system. This way, he could live happily ever after without doing much. Obviously, he would work hard to improve the system by adding water pipes. However, he would make money 24/7 without doing anything. He had achieved freedom.

This is a perfect example of the game plan of mediocrity versus the game plan of wealth. Game plan 2 versus game plan 3. On one game plan, you keep working hard and never really increase in freedom or wealth. On the other game plan, you work hard to create a system that will eventually make you money without you being there.

You see, people on this game plan build systems that automatically do everything for them. This results in time-detachment, the crucial ingredient I talked about earlier. And, with the ingredient of time-detachment, we can achieve true freedom.

Now, I've already talked about time-detachment and I'll be talking about systems later. For now, though, just realize that this game plan is a great way to achieve freedom - financially and timewise.

LIFE

On this game plan, we think about life in a completely different way than on the other two game plans. We value our life in another way and we measure our successes in another way. To people on this game plan, life is about a lot more than status, titles, degrees, manager positions, and high salaries.

Here are some of the things people on this game plan value a lot:

IMPACT

People on this game plan value impact and legacy.. *a lot*. On this game plan, we believe in helping others and actually making a difference. We want a big funeral. We want millions of people around the world to show up to our funeral and say "because of this person, my life has been so much better." Even if it's people we've never met. We want to be remembered by a lot of people because we did something for them that they won't forget.

This desire for legacy and impact is why you see some people stay motivated their entire lives while others can't get out of bed in the morning. **When we're working on something bigger than ourselves, something that will make a huge impact on people who'll never be able to return the favor, that's when we'll be the most motivated.** Because, now you're not just working to achieve your own selfish pleasures, you're working to help a ton of people improve their lives.

You see, working hard to get a nice car can be great. However, working hard to feed homeless children is so much more motivating. Working hard to take a vacation to Hawaii can be great. But imagine working hard to take your depressed friend on a tour around the world to give him a spark of excitement and eventually get back on his feet. Which goal would be the most motivating for you?

You see, reasons are what motivates us. The reason people on this game plan are so incredibly motivated is not because they were born that way. It's because their reasons for working are so much bigger than to get a simple promotion or a 3% pay raise.

"When your why is big enough you will find your how." - *Les Brown*

"Reasons come first. Answers come second." - *Jim Rohn*

CONTRIBUTION

We value contribution for the same reasons we value impact and legacy. When contribution is the goal, you'll be a lot more motivated. You'll also feel significantly more confident because you know what you're doing is for the sake of others.

How often do you feel grateful for you having both your legs? Probably not very often. Why? Because you've gotten used to having them. Same thing when you get the new iPhone. You're happy about it at first but then, after a few days, you've gotten used to it and you're not really grateful anymore.

Believe it or not, it's the same thing with expensive cars, a nice house, etc. These materialistic pleasures are great but, eventually, they'll stop fulfilling you. This is why you see a lot of depressed rich people. People on this game plan realize that selfish pleasures can only take you so far.

On this game plan, we want to do more for others. Our focus and our mission is to do something great for others and make a positive impact on their lives. Contribution is what drives us.

So, am I not interested in exotic cars, beach houses, etc.? Interested is a huge fucking understatement. My mouth waters when I think about these things. I have a great desire for these materialistic pleasures and I promise you, one day, I'll acquire all of them. No doubt about it.

What I'm suggesting, however, is that your materialistic pleasures should be results, or by-products, of you making a positive impact and helping others. It shouldn't be your purpose and it should definitely not be your sole reason for working. **The funny, ironic thing about focusing on impact and contribution over materialistic pleasures is that, this way, we'll actually be able to acquire the materialistic pleasures faster.**

So, if you want the fast cars, the sick parties all over the world, the amazing house, and the huge bank account, start focusing on improving other people's lives and *make an impact.*

TIME

On the other two game plans, especially the second one, time isn't valued. Not compared to a lot of other things, at least. On this third game plan, however, maximizing one's time is one of the main focuses. You see, valuing one's time is one of the most crucial aspects of this game plan. If you don't value your time, you'll be destroyed by the select few who do.

> *"I've never met a rich person who didn't value his time, and I've never met a poor person who did." - Peter Voogd*

On game plan 1 and 2, we value money over time and we make trades accordingly by giving away our time in exchange for money. On this third game plan, however, we actually value time more than money. We trade money in exchange for time. **To get** truly wealthy, you shouldn't trade your time for money. You should use your money to save time.

Why is this? Why is time worth so much more than money? Because you can always get more money, but you can never get more time. Time is a nonrenewable resource. Right now, you are the youngest you'll ever be. Never will you ever be younger than you are at this exact moment. However, there is a very good chance you'll one day have more money than you do right now.

Well, if you don't trade your time away for money, how would you ever make money? I'd love to get into that right here. I won't, though, because there's gonna be a lot about that later. Just realize that time is your most important resource and you should treat it like every hour is worth $10,000. Don't expect to get wealthy by trading it away for $16 an hour.

GROWTH

Improving, growing, learning, studying, etc. On game plan 1 and 2, all this ends when we graduate. "Yes! I never have to read a book again in my life!" On this third game plan, however, growing is an all-time thing. It's something we do from when we're born till we're dead. We always sharpen our skills, improve as a person, learn new things, etc. Every day is an opportunity to improve and get better.

I'm gonna stop breathing before I stop growing.

On this game plan, we strive to always be better than we were yesterday. Imagine what would happen if you improved by 1% every single day. Within a year, you would've improved by 365%. Do this for 10 years, and you can't even imagine the possibilities. This is without compounded interest. If we put that in the equation, you'd improve by an unbelievable amount!

I'm not gonna go deep into this topic here because there's an entire chapter about it later. However, I want you to understand the power of always improving and growing. Can you see how someone who grows from age 6 to 90 will outperform and achieve a lot more than someone who grows from age 6 to 22?

If you decide to always grow and always be better than yesterday, you'll without a doubt get ahead of 95% of people. You'll become so much more, which will allow you to do so much more, which will allow you to give so much more, which will allow you to *have* so much more. Always grow, even if it's just a little bit. Always be better than yesterday. This is the most powerful commitment you can make to yourself and it will, without a doubt, change everything.

BEST VERSION

Another very obvious characteristic about people on this game plan is that they're always striving to be the best version of themselves. With every decision, every choice, and every action, they're asking themselves what the best version of themselves would do. This desire to be as much as possible is what makes them so extraordinary and exceptional in everything they do.

I've been obsessed with this my entire life. If I know I can do something, then that's what I expect of myself. I can perform incredibly well and still be extremely disappointed. I can also perform what other people might call a disaster while still being extremely proud. It's all about how much of my potential I'm reaching.

As a child, when I played sports, video games, or other sorts of competition, I'd have two very different ways of reacting to a loss. Sometimes I'd walk up to the competitor with a smile on my face and thank him for a wonderful game. Other times, I'd cry, yell, etc. I would feel extremely disappointed with myself.

So, *what was the difference?* Well, the differentiator that determined my reaction was whether or not I had lived up to my full potential. Whether or not I had performed the best I possibly could. **I'd much rather lose while reaching my full potential than I'd win while only giving 90%.**

A lot of people are telling me that I can't be perfect, which is true. No one can. However, if I know I can be 78% perfect, then I better not be 72%. If I know I'm capable of getting 113 points, then I better not get 104. If I know I can do something, then there's no excuse for not doing it.

You see, people on this game plan, including myself, often have a lot of competitors. We care about being good compared to others. If we didn't, the marketplace would destroy us. What many of us care a lot more about, though, is being good compared to our own potential. Being good compared to the best version of ourselves.

In school, I'd sometimes be extremely happy with a shitty grade. Other times, I'd go home disappointed because I made one mistake on my math test, even though I achieved the best possible grade. I don't care about others telling me I did good. I care about giving it 100%. I care about reaching my *full potential.*

Don't compare yourself to others. Compare yourself to the absolute best version of yourself. Compare yourself to your capabilities and *your* potential.

By the way, I'm working on a huge project that will change the game completely for everyone involved. I'll make further announcements on this in the <u>Cure Mediocrity group on Facebook</u>

so make sure you're in there. The slogan for this project will be *Don't Waste Your Potential.*

Money and Wealth

So, we've talked about how people on this game plan view life. This subchapter is about how people on this game plan manage money. A lot of people will not accept that things can be done this way. The reason for this is that it'll go against a lot of the things they've been taught their entire lives. If you listen with an open mind, however, you'll be introduced to a whole new way of becoming wealthy.

You see, instead of trading their time away for $16 an hour, people on this game plan build systems. They build things that'll make them money 24/7 without their presence. So, instead of getting paid $16 for their hour, they'll spend that hour creating something that will make them thousands in the long term.

A great example can be this book. Once I've written it and set up an automated marketing system, I'll have a "money machine" that will generate money 24/7. This book can be bought over and over again without me doing anything. Now, I'm definitely gonna update it and I'm obviously gonna have to make sure my marketing is working. The point I wanna make, however, is that this book just needs to be written once and it'll make me money *forever.*

If you calculate what I'm gonna make on this book within the next 15 years and then you divide that number by the hours I spent writing it, you'll see that the amount of money I make hourly is way more than some of the most lucrative professions.

Now, I'm not gonna make anything while researching for this book. I'm not gonna make anything while writing the book. I'm also not gonna make a lot of money within the first few months of publishing. Over time, though, I'll be making more money per hour with this book than I would've at a job.

This is how people on this game plan think. They don't trade their time away for money. Instead, they spend their time creating things that will produce income on their own. In other words, people on this game plan spend their time building money machines and planting money trees. Once built, these things will make the owner money without his presence or time.

These things are called assets. Businesses, systems, and investments that continuously make you money. Here are few examples:

- A book.

- An app.

- A property you rent out.

- Software that your customers pay a monthly fee for.

- A membership program.

- A business.

However, it can also be as simple as putting an arcade game in someone's bar. Customers at the bar will then play your game and you'll make money without being there. Creating and/or buying an asset doesn't have to be advanced and complicated.

The great thing about a money tree is that you can use its fruit to plant even more trees. If you rent out a property, you can save the profits. Then, when the property has provided enough profits, you can buy another one. Now you have two money machines. You can then use the profits from these two money machines to save up for a third one.

"I can't afford to invest in real estate. Where do I find the money to buy an entire property?" Well, the way you do this is by using OPM (Other People's Money). You put yourself in debt. Yes, I know you've been told that all debt is bad. However, I'm here to tell you that, without debt, you'll have a very hard time getting wealthy. You just have to understand the difference between bad debt and good debt.

Here's an example. I go to the bank and get a mortgage to be able to buy this property. The property produces $1300 every month because that's what the tenants pay for rent. It costs me $200 every month to manage the property. Out of the $1100 left, I give $800 of them to the bank to pay back my mortgage. As you can see, this property is now putting $300 in my pocket every single month without me having to do anything. Additionally, I'm paying back the mortgage with the tenants' money. I don't have to get into why it's awesome to pay off a mortgage.

I've simplified the process a lot here because I'm gonna dedicate an entire chapter to this concept later in the book. For now, though, just realize that the name of the game of wealth is income. Income doesn't have to require you to spend your time. If you build, or buy, assets, systems, and investments, you'll make money without doing anything. You can then use that money to build or buy even more assets. Keep doing this, and you'll get very wealthy! This is the way people on this game plan handle money and wealth.

MATH

As I said earlier, this book isn't just opinions and perspectives. It's based on numbers and facts. The way to get wealthy is through math. Without the numbers, it's impossible to get wealthy. This is why, on this game plan, we like to rely on things we can control instead of luck and the marketplace. We also don't like to waste time on things that clearly aren't scalable. How do we know if what we're doing will make us wealthy? Well, we look at the numbers.

On the game plan of mediocrity, we rely on a ton of unscalable, uncontrollable variables. These variables are things like our job, our salary, our hours spent, the housing market, the stock market, etc. Unfortunately, like I said earlier, very few of these are in our control. Even fewer of them are ones we can scale unlimitedly.

On this third game plan, however, the variables are as simple as:

Income = Reach * Magnitude

Or

Income = Units sold * Units profit

If you do this right and you build a system with the ingredient of scale, then you'll always be able to sell more. If not, find a way to do so. McDonald's wouldn't be scalable if it was just one burger place. Math wouldn't be on their side. However, they decided to expand via franchises and they introduced the ingredient of scale into their system.

If you want to get wealthy, you have to have math on your side and you have to control all the variables in the wealth equation. Every variable in the wealth equation of the owner needs to be controllable and scalable. If not, your results will be limited and you'll eventually get stuck spinning your wheels.

SPEEDING UP THE PROCESS

When on this game plan, we want to speed up the journey toward wealth; we don't do it by searching for some hot stock. Yeah, I'm sorry, that hot stock your broke uncle talks about will not make you a millionaire in 13 days if you just invest $500 now.

On this game plan, we realize that the road to wealth isn't through hot stocks, clever saving tricks, etc. It's through adding actual, legitimate value to the marketplace. How do we add value to the marketplace? By being valuable. How do we become valuable? By having valuable skills that can solve problems. **The way to wealth is to be valuable and to be able to do something that others will pay for.**

"The more you learn, the more you earn." - Warren Buffett

So, when those who are on the game plan of wealth want to speed up the process, we learn, improve, and grow. We sharpen our skills, learn new valuable things, or come up with other ideas to become even more valuable. We realize that the better we are, at our craft and as overall human beings, the better we'll do in life - emotionally and financially.

This is why it's so crucial that you and I continuously educate ourselves on life, money, happiness, people, and other super important and valuable aspects of life. This is also why I admire and respect you for finding this book, buying it, and reading it. Some of you might even implement what I'm talking about. By doing this, you're setting yourself up to do so much better than everyone who doesn't. Much more importantly, though, you're setting yourself up to reach more of your own potential. You're helping yourself get closer to being the best version of yourself.

Now, if this doesn't interest you, there's always room for you on the game plan of poverty. All you have to do there is buy a lottery ticket and pray. You can also choose to speed up the process the way many do it on the game plan of mediocrity. Stop drinking Starbucks, read a book telling you to invest in a 401(k) for 40 years, and then ask your broke friend for "hot stock" advice.

Growing, learning, improving, etc. is so crucial. The more you learn the more valuable you'll become to those around you. This will almost always result in more income. Whether you're on game plan 1, 2, or 3, this will help you tremendously in life. If you're on one of the first two game plans, you should still seek to always improve and become more.

Every time you learn something valuable, the value you can add to the marketplace increases. Every time that happens, you make more money.

You see, this game plan is not based on hope. It's not based on whether or not you have a job. It's working whether or not your savings enjoy a 15% interest. These are things you can't control, much less scale.

This game plan, though, is based on value. It's based on variables that you can control, including your skills and your ideas. On this game plan, if you do what it takes to win, you'll win. On the game plan of mediocrity, if you do what it takes to win, you'll have a 5% chance of "winning" (meaning an acceptable retirement). I'm sorry, I'm just not sold on that plan. I want to get punched in the face if I screw up and I want to achieve everything I desire if I do well. That's what I love about this game plan. Whether or not you win is up to you.

Now, there's obviously a lot of things that can happen, even if you're on this game plan. I would never tell you that, by following this game plan, you'd have a 100% chance of becoming a millionaire in two years. What I can promise you, however, is that if there are people out there who want to pay you for what you can do for them, you can make money. So, your job on this game plan is to really make sure you're always adding value to the marketplace.

You might go all in on starting a paper company. A few years in, you realize that paper is dying because everything is getting digitalized. First of all, that's your fault for not thinking about that. Second of all, you would've learned so much about starting a company. You can then take this experience and use it to start another, this time *profitable*, business.

Again, I don't wanna promise you anything. However, look at the numbers and the facts. If people want your value, they'll pay you. So, if you continue to add massive value to the marketplace, you'll inevitably end up very successful. Especially if you learn from every mistake and you don't give up. Eventually, it'll happen.

CONCLUSION/CHAPTER BULLET POINTS

Here are some characterizing viewpoints, perspectives, principles, etc. of people on this game plan - the game plan of wealth:

- We feel a huge sense of urgency about life. We know time is very scarce and valuable. Because of this, we always seek to get the most out of it.

- We value time much more than we value money.

- We don't buy money for time. We buy time for money.

- Traditional education (school) *can* be useful. Real education, however, is always useful and it's a necessity for a great life - *emotionally and financially.*

- We'd rather plant a money tree that'll make money 24/7 instead of trade away our time every time we want to make money.

- We like having more than one income stream.

- We use the profits from our money machines to create, acquire, or buy even more.

- Not all debt is bad. Good debt is crucial and necessary when generating wealth.

- Compound interest is great... but only when we already have a large sum of money. We don't rely on compound interest to create wealth, we rely on it to sustain and increase it.

- Scalability, control, and time-detachment are crucial. If the project doesn't have these three ingredients, we're not very interested. Unless we can add these ingredients.

- Freedom over security. *Always.*

- We want the variables in our wealth equation to be determined by ourselves, not uncontrollable third parties. Units sold * unit profit.

- We use math in our game plan, instead of luck and hope.

- If we want to make more money, we better add more value. We do this by always improving and learning.

- We want the luxurious lifestyle. However, we want that to be a by-product of helping a ton of people.

- We value impact and legacy *a lot.*

- We don't hate on successful people. We get inspired and learn from them.

- We might compare ourselves to others. Our focus, however, is to compare ourselves to the best version of ourselves.

- Status, great schools, and an advanced degree don't mean shit compared to a person's character.

- We respect people on other game plans and other roads to wealth.

- We'll always treat the janitor and the CEO equally.

[9]

THE FOUR INCOME STREAMS

There are millions of different income streams. Everything from being a fortune cookie writer to being a dog surfing instructor. When it comes to making money, only your imagination can limit you. I'd rather take a nap on the bottom of a lake than talk about every single income stream out there. What I can do, however, is categorize the income streams into four sections.

1. Having a job - employed

2. Having a job - self-employed

3. Owning a system - business owner

4. Owning an investment - investor

You see, there are four different types of income streams. These four types of income streams are very different in every way. Not only in the way we make money or how much we make, but also the way we think about life. Every one of these income streams can be awesome and they can also suck. People can get rich with all of them and people can also be poor with all of them. However, two of them definitely have advantages when it comes to generating wealth.

Again, I'm not here to tell you which ones are "correct." I'm just here to inform you that they all exist. Because, you see, the first two income streams are talked about by everyone. The system makes sure we're perfectly prepared for these two types of income streams. Society makes sure we believe that these two ways of making money are the only options.

This is not right because, even though a lot of people fit best in the first two categories, some of us prefer the last two options. For this reason, I think it would be fair to teach everyone about all of them and then let people make their own decision instead of society making the decision for us.

By the way, something very crucial to realize is that you can, and probably should, leverage more than one of these categories. The average millionaire has 7 different income streams. These income streams do not have to come from the same category. I leverage 3 of these types of income streams and I definitely suggest you leverage at least two of them.

1. JOB: EMPLOYED

The first income stream is having a job. To be employed by someone who then pays you for your time and effort. By leveraging this income stream, we get paid to make someone else a lot of money. We often get a very small portion of the amount of money we make for our employer. Additionally, we sacrifice our time because we get paid by the number of hours we work. So, the more we sacrifice our time, and the more effort we put into making our employer a lot of money, the more money this income stream will generate.

If we want to strengthen this income stream and increase the amount of money it generates, we'll often work harder, hope for a pay raise, or both. We'll find a way to make our employer even more money. This way, we'll be more valuable and when the value we can add to someone increases, we'll get paid more.

VIEWS AND PERSPECTIVES

Having a job and being employed isn't just about your method of generating income. It's actually about a lot more. Often times, it's about how you view life. It's what you value and it's about your perspectives when it comes to things like freedom, risk, work, etc. Generating income this way says a lot about your personality and your values.

It's no surprise that this income stream is best for people who value security, safety, and comfort. It's a very simple way of generating income. It might take up a lot of time, it might be exhausting, and it might not produce a lot of money, but it's simple and very straight forward. It's very secure and there's not a lot of risk... as long as you don't get fired, that is.

Unfortunately, since there are not many things you can control, there's not a lot of possibilities for scale. The only things you can do to scale this kind of income stream is to work harder or work more hours. This obviously won't lead to freedom. However, people leveraging this income stream have often accepted that. They've often accepted that freedom and prosperity is not possible when they have this desire for safety, comfort, and simplicity.

Employed people are often people who avoid risk at all cost. They look at risk and possibility for failure as something horrible that must be avoided. Failure and mistakes cannot happen because, if they do, it means we're not good enough. The less mistakes one makes, the better that person is.

This is a very destructive and messed up way of thinking.

Avoiding failure, mistakes, and risks as a way to get ahead is possibly the most ironic, impractical, and counterproductive method there is. Do this, and you'll be very disappointed with your results.

This fear of failure, the fear of being embarrassed in front of friends and relatives, but more importantly, oneself, is what prevents so many people from following their dreams. This fear of failure and risk is what attracts people to this income stream instead of some of the more lucrative ones.

So, why do most people avoid risks? Why do most people hate making mistakes instead of embracing them? How come people don't look at mistakes as stepping stones to success since, after all, we learn the most by failing?

There's a very simple explanation for this. The reason we look at mistakes as these horrible things that must be avoided is because that's what we've been taught since we were 5 years old. We've been brainwashed to think that the less mistakes we make, the better we are. This is what we learn in school.

Now, I don't know about you, but when I received my results from a math test in school, it wasn't measured by my thought-process throughout the test. It wasn't measured by how quickly I answered the questions. It wasn't measured by my understanding of the materials and it certainly wasn't measured by my way of thinking. No, it was measured by how many mistakes I had made. For every mistake I made, I'd get a worse grade.

This is a messed up way of teaching.

I remember as a child, I was super excited about this subject in school. I don't know if you have this exact subject in the US but the closest thing would be social studies. I was super excited and I would raise my hand almost every time the teacher asked us something. Every single time, I'd have this very informative, super correct answer. Except for a few times, like 1 out 25, where I'd have the answer wrong.

It didn't really bother me because I learned every time I was wrong. I didn't really mind. Until I got my grades...

Now, I received a decent grade. However, when I found that I had received a worse grade than one of my friends, I got so confused. She almost never said anything and, when she did, it wasn't as informative as my answers.

So, I talked to my teacher about this and here's what he said: "Daniel, almost everything you're saying is brilliant. Unfortunately, sometimes, you raise your hand without being 100% sure that your answer is correct. Don't just guess or try, have the facts. If you didn't make these mistakes, you'd definitely get a better grade."

Guess what, I didn't raise my hand once the rest of that year. I was so pissed. More importantly, though, I was afraid of making mistakes because, clearly, the less mistakes you make, the better you are.

Now, I know a lot of people might be shaking their heads saying, "I mean, obviously, if you make a mistake you get a worse grade, duh."

However, I really don't believe that punishing people for every mistake, making them terrified to fail, is the right way to give a child feelings of courage, confidence, and ambition. I really don't.

I could write an entire book about failure and adversity. This is beyond the scope of this book, though. However, it's crucial to realize the reason this income stream is so appealing to so many people. It's because we get convinced that mistakes are something to avoid. It's really not. We need to embrace failure and we need to welcome risk.

So, to everyone who wouldn't dare think about leveraging other income streams than this one, I challenge you to welcome risk. I challenge you to be less afraid of making mistakes. Don't be afraid of taking chances. Don't jump off a cliff, but take a lot of calculated risks. Risks that will push you further toward your dreams of wealth, prosperity, and freedom.

HOW TO GET RICH THIS WAY

Honestly, I'm not a huge fan of getting rich entirely by having a job. The reason for this is that a job isn't scalable. Also, if your job is your only income stream, you'll have no income once you stop working. This is not ideal if you desire true freedom and wealth.

So, if you want to get rich by leveraging this income stream, I highly recommend combining it with at least one of the other income streams. The best income stream to combine with having a job is definitely investing in assets. What you can do here is take a percentage of what you earn and then use that money to acquire assets.

Now, I'm not talking about putting your money in some random 401(k). I'm talking about buying actual assets. I'm talking about buying a money tree. This can be real estate, stocks, etc. It can also be as simple as buying an arcade game and asking your local bar if you can set it up with them. As long as it keeps putting money in your pocket every month. Then, what you can do is use those profits to buy another money tree. Eventually, your automatic profits, also called passive income, will exceed your expenses. You can then quit your job or, at least, work fewer hours.

Now, before you take on as big a task as buying a property or something like that, you'll obviously want to educate yourself on the topic. If real estate is what you want to invest in, you should educate yourself until you know what you're doing. If you buy a piece of property by guessing, you'll end up in crap to your knees.

Investing in real estate and other assets is far beyond the scope of this book. However, please realize how huge an opportunity it is to invest in assets. This is how most wealthy people got wealthy and you can do it too, even though you're in a job.

So, to sum it up. A job has limits and it cannot make you wealthy and free on its own. It can, however, be used as a tool to generate the income you need to acquire assets. These assets can then make you wealthy and free. So, having a job is definitely not a bad thing. Just don't expect to get wealthy through that income stream alone.

2. JOB: SELF-EMPLOYED

The second kind of income stream is generated by being self-employed. As self-employed, we make money for ourselves. We provide some kind of service for a customer and, in return, we get paid by the customer. Because we're self-employed, we get to keep everything that's left after our expenses.

As self-employed, we're still trading time away for money, though. Often times, our hour is worth more as self-employed than when we're in a job because we get 100% of the profits. However, we can't get around the fact that we're still making the time for money trade. As we all know by now, trading time for money isn't scalable because there are too many limitations.

Here are some examples of self-employed jobs:

- Lawyer

- Psychologist

- Professional dog walker

- Designer

- Personal trainer

If self-employed, these people get paid by session or by project. In other words, they get paid when they work.

This income stream can be a bit more overwhelming than an employed job. It can seem challenging and difficult to rent a place, set up a private practice, and handle all the papers, taxes, etc. If done properly, however, the income can be pretty lucrative. Especially compared to a normal job.

If we, as self-employed, want to strengthen our income stream and increase the money it generates, we have two options.

Improve our skills and services. This way, we can charge our customers more.

Obtain more customers. This way, we can.. well, I don't have to talk about why more customers is a great way to increase income.

VIEWS AND PERSPECTIVES

"If you want something done right, you should do it yourself."

This is the mentality of a lot of self-employed people. Self-employment is very appealing to the person who wants to do things himself. They don't want other people to have anything to do with the amount of money they make.

In my opinion, this way of thinking can be very dangerous and it can be detrimental to one's success, wealth, and freedom. However, I get where people are coming from. A lot of the people who leverage this stream of income like to depend on themselves entirely. They want to get rewarded when they do great work.

The downside to this is that self-employed people ONLY get rewarded when they do great work. With the last two streams of income, we get rewarded every minute of every day, regardless of what we're doing. As self-employed, however, we only get paid when we work. Yes, we might make more money than a regular employed person with a job, but we're still trading time away for money. We do this because people on this game plan are terrified of letting other people help them. At a job, we're afraid to make mistakes ourselves. As self-employed, we're afraid others will make mistakes, so we don't ask them for help.

People leveraging this income stream are often inspired by entrepreneurship and the idea of starting a business. They feel that being self-employed is the step between a regular job and a business, which I agree with. A lot of self-employed people aren't really ready to start a real business.

Going from self-employed to business owner requires one to build a system. Building a system requires hiring people. This can be challenging for the guy who wants to do everything by himself. This is why there's a lot of people who want to get wealthy by owning a business but then become self-employed instead of becoming a business owner.

How to Get Rich This Way

Now, just like with the first income stream, I suggest combining this one with investing in assets. Use the profits from your self-employed job to acquire, buy, or create money machines that'll continuously make you money. Then, use the profits from those money machines to acquire even more of them.

Another thing I'd like to challenge you to consider, if you're currently relying on this kind of income stream, is to automate things. Take your little self-employed job and turn it into a business system. This can be, for example, hiring five chiropractors and turn your little private practice into a clinic. It can also be as simple as hiring an accountant to automate your finances.

How you automate your self-employed job and turn it into a business depends on what you're doing. A professional dog walker would have to do it in a different way than a lawyer would, obviously. I can't tell you what your first automating step should be unless I know your business, your skills and your ideas.

However, oftentimes the question really answers itself. "What can/should I automate?" If you spend a lot of your time and money on acquiring customers, hire a salesperson or a marketer. If you spend a lot of time doing your taxes and other financial stuff, hire an accountant or a bookkeeper.

Automating things is the greatest, most powerful way to scale.

Just like with a regular job, it can be difficult to get wealthy and achieve freedom without combining this income stream with another. If, however, you decide to use a self-employed job to be able to acquire assets and one day turn your job into an automated system, you'll definitely have the opportunity and the possibility to get wealthy. Don't rely on this income stream entirely, but leverage it as a tool to acquire assets.

3. SYSTEM: BUSINESS OWNER

"Your goal is to own a system and have people work that system for you." - Robert Kiyosaki

This income stream is leveraged by people on the game plan of wealth. The income is generated by a system. A system that works continuously without your presence. This is extremely scalable, controllable, and doesn't require your time. So, as you can see, this income stream has all three ingredients.

In his book, *Rich Dad's Cashflow Quadrant*, Robert Kiyosaki gives his opinion on a proper money system. If you can disappear for a year and then come back to find your business making even more money than when you left, that's when you've built a proper system.

Now, in my opinion, this might be a bit of an overkill. However, I am deeply in love with the idea. I love the idea that you can build something once and then it makes money and grows, makes money and grows, continuously... *on its own*. The idea that what you're building could potentially make you money without you touching it for an entire year. This will provide freedom and it'll make you so incredibly wealthy.

So, yeah, this income stream is really a money machine. You create something that'll eventually function on its own and then you just enjoy the reaps over and over again. You can then choose to put effort into scaling it, selling it, or spend the profits on another project, e.g. a new system.

Here's an example of a business system:

1. Step 1. I create a $197 course on equestrian yoga (yep, that's yoga on a horse).

2. Step 2. I create an automated 5-mail email series, while making sure to properly promote my course in the last email.

3. Step 3. I write a $19 book about equestrian yoga. In this book, I encourage people to sign up for my free email series.

4. Step 4. I create something extremely valuable and turn it into some kind of free PDF. This can be as simple as "3 tips that'll make you a better equestrian yoga practitioner." In this free PDF, I'm gonna encourage people to buy my book.

5. Step 5. I market and advertise my free PDF. This can be done in a ton of different ways. My favorite is through social media.

6. Step 6. I optimize every step of the system until, eventually, I spend less on acquiring a customer than I make. This means I'll profit every time I acquire a new customer. I can then pay someone to manage my Facebook ads and make sure that my ads continuously get updated for maximum results.

As you can see, I just reverse-engineered (that's planning backward) a business system. More and more customers will keep going through this system from step 5 to step 1. It might cost me $0.64 to acquire a customer while I make $1.38. That's $0.74 of profit every time a customer goes through my system. And, because of my automated advertising, customers will continuously go through the system.

Obviously, this is just an example of how it can be done. This was not meant to be a guide on how to create the perfect business system because, again, that'd require a whole book.

Anyway, this kind of income stream is automatic, scalable, controllable, and it doesn't require much of your time once it's built. I am very much in love with this kind of income stream. If you want to get really, truly wealthy, this is definitely something you should consider. I know it might seem overwhelming, but you can definitely build a business system yourself. I'll admit that my previous example was a little simplified. However, the process is often pretty simple.

VIEWS AND PERSPECTIVES

So, what kind of people does this income stream appeal to? Well, this income stream is usually leveraged by people on the third game plan, the game plan of wealth. It's appealing to people who want more than a regular job. It's for people who hate wasting their potential and they feel like they would do so in a job. This income stream is for everyone wanting more than to just get by, living paycheck to paycheck.

This income stream is for those who desire true wealth, prosperity, and freedom.

People leveraging this income stream are often not afraid of risk. Instead, we welcome it. Now, we're definitely not reckless or careless. With this income stream, we always want to think long and hard about what we're doing. We will not build a system before we know what we're doing. However, a little risk does not prevent us from taking action, at all. As long as we always think before we act, we don't mind risk.

"In life, there's risk and there's recklessness. Risk is always okay and it's always meant to be pursued. Recklessness is really dangerous and really stupid. It should always be avoided." - Casey Neistat

With this income stream, risk is inevitable. The people leveraging this kind of income stream are often not just welcoming risk, they're embracing it. We realize that, without risk, mistakes, and failure, we'll never achieve great things. With this income stream, we have to understand that **extraordinary results never happen in one's comfort zone.** We have to do things that scare us. We have to take the shot even though we might miss.

This income stream is very appealing to people who like adventure, thrills, and excitement. There are a lot of boring things that you'll be doing over and over. Trust me, though, there's nothing as exciting as building businesses. There are so many fun and exciting things about building businesses and creating money systems. So, if you like excitement and adventure, you'll definitely enjoy this income stream.

So, the first two income streams are, for the most part, secure and safe. This can be great, but **safety will always limit opportunity.** This third income stream, however, can be more adventurous. Because of this, there's a lot more opportunity for extraordinary results. This income stream is more about results than it is about mistakes. With this income stream, it's crucial to count our positive results instead of our mistakes and failures, because we'll be making a lot of them.

Another thing we need if we want to make this income stream function is delayed gratification.

Delayed gratification is the ability to resist the temptation for an immediate reward and wait for a later reward. Generally, delayed gratification is associated with resisting a smaller but more immediate reward in order to receive a larger or more enduring reward later.

This is probably one of the most difficult things about building a business. You have to work a lot without getting paid. Again, I've been working on this book for a very long time. I've spent so many hours on it, every single day. And how much have I been paid for these hours of hard work? Zero, nothing, nada. I've worked a ton of hours for a $0/hour rate. Imagine how much money I would've made if I had spent those hours at a normal job.

In the long-term, however, I'll make more money on this book than if I had worked at a job for $12 an hour. Think about it: every single time I sell a copy of this book, the hours I spent writing it will increase in value. So, as of this writing, I've worked a ton of hours for nothing. In the long-term, however, it will be worth it.

This is what you need to tell yourself daily while building a business. **In the long-term, it will be worth it.** For a very long time, you're spending your money, time, effort, and other resources to build something that will, hopefully, make money in the future.

This is very difficult for many and I believe this is the reason why so many people choose to get paid by the hour instead of building a system. In the future, it will definitely be worth it to build a system, a business. However, in the present, it can be challenging to work hard without getting paid immediately.

So, if you're prepared to be delayed-gratification-oriented, this is a very awesome income stream and you should definitely consider it. You have to realize that it'll be hard and that you won't make any money for a good amount of time. Once you've built the system, however, it's extremely lucrative and it'll provide freedom and wealth for the owner. With these things in mind, if you're still interested in this kind of income stream, you should definitely go for it.

> *"Eat shit for 24 months and eat caviar for the rest of your life." - Gary Vaynerchuk*

To leverage this income stream properly, you have to always think long-term and stay delayed-gratification-oriented.

HOW TO GET RICH THIS WAY

Getting rich by building systems is an advanced, overwhelming task and then it's really not. This might sound a little confusing. What I mean by this is, in a business system, there are a lot of little things that you can tweak and improve. The ideas behind all of it, however, are pretty simple.

Build something scalable and controllable that doesn't require your time once it's built. Then, use the profits to either scale your current system or to build a new one.

At first, the process might be a little slow because you're in the learning process. This is why procrastination should be avoided. The sooner you begin, the quicker you'll become good at building systems. The quicker you become good at building systems, the faster you'll get wealthy and the younger you'll be able to enjoy your freedom. This is why I cringe every time family members or friends ask me "What's the rush?" The rush is that I wanna have my freedom as young as possible. *Why wait?*

As soon as possible, educate yourself on business, entrepreneurship, and money. Then, when you're ready, build a system with the three crucial ingredients. You will not become a millionaire in 13 days. However, if you do it right, you should be able to see results eventually.

At first, you should focus on the big, important things. I see people put all of their efforts into business cards, logos, and professional websites before they serve a single customer. This is not ideal. It's better to just focus on the important things like your product and your system. Your priority is to get something up and running that helps customers and makes you money.

Then, when you start seeing results, when you have an *actual business*, that's when you can start to focus on conversion rates and other tweaks. Don't get me wrong, these things are extremely important. However, conversion optimization tweaks don't matter if you only have three people visit your website.

If there's one thing I would've loved to know when I first started with entrepreneurship, it's this: You do not need to know everything before you get started. You don't need to know everything about every step of the way before you start your journey. That's like waiting in your garage for every light between your house and your destination to turn green. It will never happen and you will never get started.

Know what you're getting yourself into, but fuck the business cards and the fancy websites. Just get started.

So, here's the process I recommend for going from nothing to wealth and freedom:

1. Study entrepreneurship, business, and money. (Never stop doing this.)

2. Find your calling: your passion and skills combined with a need you can fill for your customers.

3. Somehow sell what you're doing.

4. Build a system that sells what you're doing *on its own.*

5. Scale your system.

6. Optimize your system or repeat steps 3 to 5 with another idea.

7. Spend a portion of all profits on buying assets (real estate, stocks, etc.).

DISCLAIMER!

All these things are, at the base, pretty simple ideas. Simple, however, does not mean easy. I believe everyone can get started and I believe building systems, investing in assets, and getting rich in general, isn't that complicated. You can do this by understanding the basic principles of money. But, again, just because it's simple doesn't mean it's easy. Building a proper business system and then scaling it to a point where it will make you wealthy is not something you just do. If it was, everyone would do it. Building a business requires hard work, a lot of time, and often a lot of money, too.

If you're ready to be delayed-gratification-oriented and think long-term, you're ready to invest your time, energy, and money into building this, and you're prepared to work hard for your dreams, then I believe you can achieve extraordinary things others only dream about. You can get wealthier than you would've ever imagined. You can achieve freedom like you never thought possible.

I want you to have clear expectations, though.

There might be a lot of scam artists out there promising you that you can become a millionaire within a month by doing nothing. *It's not true.* I could write a book that promises people things like that and I'd make a lot more money than I will on this one. I'm not interested in that, though. I'm interested in getting rich, yes, that's very true. However, I would hate to be rich if I had gotten there by scamming people. Money is great but impact and legacy is what really matters to me.

So, I wanna be honest with you. Getting extremely wealthy by building money systems is real and you have the potential to do it. Lots of other people have done it. However, it does not come easy. It'll always be 100% worth it, in my opinion, but it's a rough, bumpy ride.

When going all in on building a business, I want you to remember these two things at all times:

1. If it was easy, everyone would do it.

2. It will be worth it.

4. ASSETS: INVESTOR

Like with the business system, real assets and investments are mostly leveraged by people on the game plan of wealth. People leveraging this stream of income can get results everywhere from going broke, breaking even, or getting very wealthy.

As we all know, many investors lose their money. There's one reason for that: People have no idea what they're doing so they either let others do it for them or they give it a try themselves and end up losing everything.

A wise and competent investor, however, will achieve great results in the game of money. Investing is the single best way to amass massive wealth... *if you do it right*, that is.

A good investor spends his money buying assets. These assets then generate a steady income for the owner. Also, in a lot of cases, the asset can appreciate, meaning it will increase in value. The owner can then sell the asset and profit what's called a *capital gain.*

Investors make money by buying assets with either their own money or someone else's. They then spend the profits on even more assets. There's rarely a limit on the amount of wealth investors can achieve because there are always more assets to be acquired.

I'm going to talk a lot more about investing and assets in the next chapter.

VIEWS AND PERSPECTIVES

Investors often share many of the same viewpoints and perspectives as the system owners. Often, they're the same people. A lot of investors own business systems and vice versa. And just like business owners, investors prefer that their money works for them instead of them working for money.

And, again, like with the business owners, investors have to be extremely delayed-gratification-oriented. No matter how little or how much money you have, it can be challenging to buy assets instead of buying a new car. It can be difficult to convince yourself to spend your money on a good investment instead of a bigger TV.

If you want to really leverage this income stream, though, you have to give up some materialistic pleasures at first. You can make yourself feel better by reminding yourself that investing a little now will create great results later. You can then buy a lot more materialistic pleasures in the future.

So, yeah, if you're looking to leverage this income stream, which you probably should if you wanna get truly wealthy, then you should learn to discipline yourself and become a delayed-gratification-oriented person.

How to Get Rich This Way

Investing is great. Investing multiplies your money without you having to do anything. Once you've invested in an asset, it should put money in your account while you sleep, eat, travel, etc. Your investment should be working for you 24/7. This means that, with investing, you can make a ton of money, a lot more than most jobs would pay you, while doing nothing. Additionally, investing is very controllable and extremely scalable. Investing is great.

What's crucial to realize, however, is that investing multiplies your money. This means that the effectiveness of investing depends, partially, on how much money you have. If you gain a 9% return on $1.37, you're not gonna get rich. Imagine getting a 9% return on $200,000, though.

Now, the amount of money you invest is definitely not the only variable. I'd much rather make an excellent investment with $5k than make a shitty investment with $200,000. Wouldn't you?

There are tons of variables that come into play when investing. Here are some of them:

- The amount you bought the asset for.

- The amount you can sell the asset for.

- The down payment/financing ratio (how much you put down of your own money vs how much you're borrowing).

- The amount of income the asset generates.

- The amount of expenses the asset generates.

- The amount of risk involved.

- The amount of time and work it requires from you to manage.

So, the amount of money you choose to invest is definitely not the only variable. If you're a good investor, you can definitely make a lot of money without already having much. What you have to consider, though, is that investing is multiplying your money. You can make a lot of money by multiplying a low number. However, multiplying a higher number will, without a doubt, result in even greater returns.

It's a snowball effect. If you roll a big snowball in the snow, it'll increase more in size than if you rolled a small one. Same thing with investing. Once you have money, investing can make you a *ton* more. If you don't have money, however, it can be a slower process. Especially if you're new to the investing game.

So, my advice is to start your journey toward wealth by building a business system. In the beginning, don't spend your money on investing in assets. I recommend spending every profit on scaling the system. Spend all your time, energy, and money on scaling the system as much as possible.

Then, when you have enough money for investing to be worth it, do it. Once you've built and scaled a business system big enough, you can start leveraging these profits to acquire assets. Grant Cardone, a financial legend, says that you shouldn't invest before you have $100k to invest. I don't know if I agree with the $100k but I definitely agree with the idea. Whether the number is $65k or $130k is totally up to you and your situation, though.

It doesn't have to be that much. It's totally up to you to decide when it's worth it to invest and acquire assets. Just keep these two things in mind:

It's best to begin as soon as possible.

Only invest in assets when it makes sense to do so instead of spending the money on scaling your system. Spend your money where there's the best return on investment.

So, invest when that's where your money will grow the most. My advice is to grow your business and do everything you can to scale it and boost the income it generates until it's worth it to invest in assets instead of scaling your system. You can always do both at the same time, though.

Just know that investing $3.84 with a 6% return won't make you rich. It's better to spend that money on building a system that then, eventually, will generate enough income for investing to be worth it.

This is where people on the game plan of mediocrity go wrong with the compound effect. They save a small amount of money in a very low-interest savings account and then they wait for the compound effect to make them rich. This is a brilliant idea. If you lived forever, that is. With this way of generating wealth, it takes 40 years to really scale it.

Wealthy people don't invest to create money. They leverage investing to multiply their money.

Going from absolutely no money to extreme wealth, leveraging only the compound effect, is a very slow process. This is why so many people won't get wealthy by working a job and contributing to their 401(k). Instead of increasing their income (income is king when it comes to creating wealth, by the way), they settle for their low salary and then cross their fingers and hope that the compound effect, on its own, will take their small amount of money and turn it into wealth and prosperity.

Here's an example of someone investing $1000 at a steady 8% return on investment:

After 5 years	$1.469	20 years	$4.661
10 years	$2.159	25 years	$6.848
15 years	$3.172	30 years	$10.063
35 years	$14.785	50 years	$46.902
40 years	$21.725	55 years	$68.914
45 years	$31.921	60 years	$101.257

After 65 years, you'd have $148,779 and if you, somehow, managed to let the compound effect work on your money for 75 years, it would've turned your $1,000 into $321,205. This means that the last 10 years, from 65 to 75, would provide greater profits than the other 65 years combined.

As you can see, with a low amount of money, the compound effect really sucks during the first 40 years. I agree, however, that it can make you wealthy after 65 years. Unfortunately, most people can't save for 65, or even 50, years. Yes, with enough years, compound effect can scale your money to tremendous amounts. But you don't live that many years. This way of creating wealth would be great if we had the patience to wait 50 years, which a lot of people apparently have. I just don't have that kind of patience.

Instead, how great would it be to cut the first 40 years off? How awesome would it be to just skip those years and get straight to the point where the compound effect doesn't just work, it makes you *rich*? Throw in the fact that you, with the right real estate deal, can enjoy up to 20% return on investment. Pretty damn great, huh?

Well, if you start out by building a business system, which you can often do in a few years, you can then have enough money to invest in things that would take you 40 years to save for. You'll cut the many unrewarding years off and get straight to the wealth scaling.

First, boost your income. Second, multiply your income.

This is how top people, the wealthiest on the planet, do it. If you desire true wealth, prosperity, and freedom at a young age, you should definitely consider leveraging this way of creating wealth.

A ton of people have done this, are doing it, or will do it. You can too. It's not easy but it's pretty simple. Build a system and then scale it or build another one until you have enough money and income. Then invest that money into assets that'll make you a ton of money - without you trading your time away, of course.

Use the income from your new assets, plus your current ones, to acquire even more. Eventually, you'll be unstoppable and there'll be no limits on your possibilities for wealth and prosperity.

CHAPTER BULLET POINTS:

- Leverage more than one of the income streams. Every wealthy person has tons of income streams.

- Most people get a job because they're afraid of failing, so they pick the least risky income stream. This is happening because we, since we were children, have been raised to believe that the more mistakes we make, the less we're worth.

- Getting wealthy and achieving freedom through a job alone is very unlikely. However, you can use a job as a tool to acquire assets that can create wealth. Having a job is definitely not bad if you use it right. Just don't expect to get wealthy by a job alone.

- There's a huge difference between being self-employed and being a business owner. One trades time away for money like at a normal job. The other one makes money every minute of every day without being present.

- Building a business system is the greatest way to create massive income. Doing so is very simple. That doesn't mean it's easy, though.

- With investing, we make money work for us instead of us working for money. Our money will multiply itself and grow on its own. This is the greatest way to create wealth and achieve freedom.

- The compound effect works the best when we already have money. So, our first job is to create massive income. This can be done through building a business. Then, when we have money to invest, we can start investing and acquiring assets.

[10]

CASH FLOW &
FINANCIAL FREEDOM

Cash flow. It's not something many of us think about, much less shape our lives around. We really should, though. At least our financial lives. Cash flow, the way our money flows from the moment we earn it till the moment we spend it, and how we spend it, is a determining factor when it comes to your future success and wealth. So, to become truly wealthy, or at least financially free, we have to understand cash flow, *the way our money flows.*

Cash flow is how you manage your money, often on a monthly basis. It's how your money flows around. And, most importantly, cash flow is what'll decide if your financial situation keeps improving or worsens.

Where does your income come from? What's the first thing you do with it once you receive your income? What do you buy? What are your expenses?

Does your financial situation improve every month? Does your net worth keep increasing? *By how much?* Are you becoming more and more free - financially and timewise? Do you get further and further into debt? Is it good debt or bad debt?

Your cash flow is what determines all of these things. The answers to these questions are determined 127 times more by your cash flow than it's determined by your salary. A 2% pay raise doesn't mean shit compared to an improvement in your cash flow.

When it comes to generating wealth, income is king. What you do once the money is in your hands, however, is 10 times as important. This is where most people screw up.

With the right cash flow, the right flow of money, we'll get wealthier and wealthier. Our net worth will keep increasing and we'll constantly get closer to our goals of financial freedom.

The opposite will happen with a bad cash flow, *a bad flow of money.* We'll keep getting in more and more bad debt. We'll keep getting more and more stressed, financially and emotionally, because we have to work harder and harder to survive. We end up ruining all chances of financial freedom and wealth because we keep worsening our financial situation.

Unfortunately, most people have shitty cash flows. Most people's cash flow is making wealth a very improbable outcome - and they don't even realize it! The flow of money that most people have is one of the reasons that so few actually become wealthy. Because we have a very inefficient flow of money. A *futile* cash flow.

This is especially true for people on the game plan of mediocrity, which is a very large percentage of people.

What's crucial to realize about getting wealthy is that nothing will make up for a shitty cash flow. Especially not an increase in income. This is one of the reasons why people on the game plan of mediocrity have a hard time getting wealthy. Because every time they want to become wealthier, instead of working on their cash flow, their game plan, etc., they work on getting a 2% or 3% pay raise.

This pay raise doesn't really help because they don't have a proper cash flow. Often, with a terrible flow of money, an increase in income will actually worsen one's financial situation.

"Making more money will not solve your problems if cash flow management is your problem." - *Robert Kiyosaki*

If you want to get wealthy, you definitely need to boost your income. Because, again, *income is king*. However, you have to realize that, with a shitty flow of money, the income will be misused and it won't provide you with the results you desire. Income and cash flow go hand in hand because both suck without the other.

A huge amount of income won't do you much good if you misuse your money. An awesome flow of money won't do much if you don't have any money. Together, however, they're great. A decent amount of income and a proper cash flow will, when combined, result in great wealth.

So, yeah, a proper cash flow is a crucial part of getting wealthy. The way you manage your money, from when you make it till it's out of your hands again, is determining your future financial success, along with many other things in this book, of course. Cash flow says a lot about whether or not you'll become wealthy and *how fast*. Unfortunately, most people's cash flow is pretty inefficient.

THE CASH FLOW OF MEDIOCRITY

The cash flow of mediocrity is, surprisingly, often leveraged by people on the game plan of mediocrity. This cash flow is leveraged by almost everyone you know. *Why?* Because, like with everything else mediocre, we become programmed by society to believe that this is the way to do it.

And, as with everything else on the game plan of mediocrity, this cash flow, this *flow of your money*, will not make you financially free and it will definitely not make you wealthy. If it, in some mysterious cases, should happen to make someone wealthy, it would take many, many years.

For most of the people leveraging this cash flow, their financial situation actually worsens with time. *Why?* Because their monthly cash flow ends in more bad debt and liabilities. With a bad cash flow like this, that continuously ends in negative numbers, it doesn't matter how much money you make. **A bad cash flow will ruin a janitor's finances as well as a doctor's.**

A TYPICAL MEDIOCRE CASH FLOW

1. A job. The first step of the typical mediocre cash flow is a job, either employed by someone else or as being self-employed. This is how most people start their cash flow. We often get this money as a salary because someone is "rewarding" us for doing a piece of work.

2. Taxes. Taxes are the next step of the typical mediocre cash flow. We pay a huge percentage of our incomes to taxes, often before we even see the money in our accounts. This means that, not only do we receive a very limited amount of money from our jobs, we actually have to pay a huge chunk of it to the govern-

ment. With this cash flow, we pay a big chunk of an already low income before we even get to see or touch the money.

3. Expenses. Now, at this point of the cash flow, many people may put a little chunk of what's left into a savings, which is great. A big part of the money we have at this point, however, will be spent on expenses. So, after we pay a huge chunk of the little income we make at a job, we spend a big part of what's left. We spend this huge part of our income on stuff like mortgages, car payments, etc. Often, at this point, there's not a whole lot of money left.

4. Fun. Now, if there's any money left at this point, this is where we can have a little fun. We can finally spend the leftovers, the last 3-5%, of what we actually made. We can spend this on a nice dinner out, a mini trip with the family, or whatever one decides to do with his money to have fun. However, most people decide to buy liabilities with their "fun" money. This can be a new TV, a new phone, or some other gadget that will actually cost money to own - not to mention it will *decrease in value*, until it's worth absolutely nothing. When we're done buying liabilities with the small amount of money we have left after taxes and expenses, we'll have spent *everything*.

5. More fun. Wait, didn't we already use up all our of money? Yes, we did. Yet, most people leveraging this income flow will, at this point, not be done spending. You see, most people aren't satisfied with the leftovers from taxes and expenses, which is very understandable. Unfortunately, what often happens is that one spends *a little bit more.* Left unsatisfied by the meager bit of money we have left for fun, we spend a little extra, thus putting ourselves in debt. We see it all the time. This can be everything from a night out that you couldn't afford, putting you $100 in

credit card debt, to taking out a loan to buy a second car. The problem with this is, by doing that, we just added more expenses to the next couple of months or, in the case of buying a new car, *years*. This means that we'll have even less money to spend on fun next month, which often results in taking on even more debt...and the vicious cycle continues.

Spoiler alert: *This cash flow will not make you wealthy.*

Can you see how no matter how high an income you have, it's very improbable to actually get wealthy this way? Can you see how even highly paid doctors can get financially frustrated and stressed when following this cash flow? This method will hardly make you wealthy. Often, it just makes people stressed and it takes this awesome thing called money and turns it into a problem. This cash flow will turn money into something you're always frustrated about.

There are three things that can happen when following this cash flow, depending on how you spend the small leftovers:

1. You spend the leftovers on fun. Unfortunately, you're not satisfied with the small chunk of money you have left after taxes and expenses. So, you buy things you simply cannot afford. You do this by taking on credit card debt and/or taking loans. Often, a lot of the "fun" you're gonna buy for the loans you take are actually liabilities. So, you take a loan, which is now a liability because you'll pay it back every month, and you spend it on acquiring a new TV that costs money to own and will only depreciate in value. You'll keep doing this every month and you'll keep having less and less money left for fun. This will lead to more and more debt every month, which again will worsen your next month's situation. In my opinion, this is a very unfortunate cash flow. You will, most of the time, end up in debt, frustration, and

stress. If you want to choose one of the cash flows of mediocrity, I recommend one of the next two.

2. You spend the leftovers on fun. You get the new pair of shoes that you can finally afford or maybe you get the new iPhone. However, you do not spend more. When your bank account says stop, you actually stop. You pay your taxes, pay your expenses, and then spend what's left. Now, unless you start making millions at your job, which is possible, you might have a hard time getting truly wealthy by doing this. You'll keep working at your job and you'll keep having fun with the leftovers. Nothing will improve unless you get a pay raise, which will result in a little bit more money to have fun with. This, by the way, is what most people do. Ask your friends and family. They're probably managing their money like this.

3. You spend the leftovers, after taxes and expenses, on acquiring assets and/or building money systems. Eventually, you'll begin getting on the right track and, at some point, you'll definitely have a shot at wealth. If you consistently spend the leftovers on improving your situation instead of worsening it, you can definitely get wealthy. Most people don't, though. It's definitely possible to get wealthy through a job if you spend everything you can on acquiring assets, like I talked about in the last chapter. No matter which cash flow you decide to use, there will always be people who got extremely wealthy that way and there'll always be people who lost everything. There's always an exception to the rule. You will find people who became rich by following the traditional, mediocre way of managing money. You'll also find people who screwed up in entrepreneurship and by leveraging the following cash flow.

It's crucial, however, to look at numbers and statistics. With this mediocre cash flow, math is obviously against us. The numbers are not in our favor. Where as when you look at the game plan of wealth and the cash flow I'll be talking about next, you can see that the numbers are on our side. You can see, by looking at numbers and facts, that it's more probable to get wealthy this way than with the mediocre way.

So, getting wealthy with a mediocre cash flow is definitely possible. But, since math - one of the most important parts of creating wealth - is against us, we'll have a very small chance of doing so. Also, if we manage to get wealthy this way, it'd take a lot more time than it would with the next cash flow I'm gonna talk about.

THE CASH FLOW OF WEALTH

With the cash flow of mediocrity, we either get further and further into debt, we stay the same, or we very slowly get a little bit wealthier. With the cash flow of wealth, however, we increase our wealth and increase our net worth continuously while we move closer and closer to our goals of wealth, freedom, and the world-class lifestyle.

We do this a lot faster than with any other cash flow.

A TYPICAL CASH FLOW OF WEALTH

1. Assets. We might get some of our income from a job, either as employed or as self-employed. Especially in the beginning, when we're first starting to leverage this kind of cash flow. With time, however, we'll begin getting a bigger and bigger percentage of our income from assets - money systems and investments. Eventually, we can stop working at our jobs because our assets provide

enough income for us to live how we want to. There's no limit on the amount of assets we can own. So, there'll never be a limit on how much money we can make. This is why leveraging this kind of cash flow is so scalable.

2. Acquiring assets. With the cash flow of mediocrity, we spend a large chunk of our income on taxes, often before we even see the money. With this cash flow, however, we spend our money on acquiring new assets. We spend our money on investments and/or on building/scaling a business system. How is this possible? How can we spend our money on assets before paying taxes? Well, this process is a little complicated, making it difficult for me to explain everything here. Like many of the other topics in this book, it would need an entire book to be explained properly. What I can tell you, however, is that this process is done through corporations. With a corporation, we get taxed on our profits. So, what we can do to avoid taxes is to spend everything on scaling our system. This way, there'll be no profits which means no taxes. Let's say I buy a chair for $20 and I sell it for $55. That's $35 of taxable money. If I spend that $35 on an advertisement that'll scale my system, there'll be no profits. This way, we take our money and spend a huge chunk of it on scaling, building, or acquiring new assets. We do this BEFORE paying taxes. This way we'll scale our wealth much faster than anyone paying taxes first. You see, because of that $35 advertisement, we might have $62 in profits the next month, which we'll then spend on something that'll scale our business. With a corporation, we can avoid a big percentage of taxes and we can spend our money on scaling our wealth. Warren Buffett, one of the richest men in America, is spending a much smaller percentage of his money on taxes than his secretary is. This is because he's a master at taxes.

3. Expenses. When we've spent a lot of our money on acquiring more assets and scaling our systems, that's when we start paying our expenses and taxes.

4. If we have more money left after paying our expenses, we'll spend the rest on fun or even more assets. Like with the cash flow of mediocrity, we might take a loan to buy something we can't afford. What we'll spend that money on, however, is a lot different than with the cash flow of mediocrity. Because, you see, with the cash flow of mediocrity, we take a loan, putting ourselves in bad debt, and we spend that borrowed money on liabilities. With the cash flow of wealth, however, we spend that money to acquire assets that'll make us more money, thus putting us in good debt that'll put money in our pockets. I'm gonna talk a lot more about good debt and bad debt later.

Now, can you see how incredibly powerful a cash flow like this is? Can you see how people following this cash flow can become very, very wealthy? Also, there's no limit on the amount of money you can make. Your wealth is extremely scalable, and it'll scale quickly. Also, as we're getting our money from assets and systems, most of it can be passive income. This cash flow is amazing and it'll make us very wealthy if we really leverage it.

I know this all might seem difficult and complicated, especially with the corporation concept. What you have to realize, though, is that a corporation is not a huge building or a giant office. It's really just a folder of papers. These papers are not difficult to handle, especially if you have some professional help. I know it might seem a little overwhelming but, if you decide to leverage this cash flow, you'll achieve great things in the game of money.

Trust me, everyone can do this and, in my opinion, everyone should.

ASSETS

So, I've been talking a lot about assets. I want everyone reading this book to really understand the power of leveraging assets as a way to get wealthy. For this reason, I want to make it crystal clear what an asset really is. Because, I mean, leveraging assets is not very useful if we have the wrong idea about what an asset is. This is the problem for many people on the game plan of mediocrity.

WHAT IT'S DEFINITELY NOT...

Again, a lot of people on the game plan of mediocrity have a very weird idea about what assets are. It's easy to have a messed up way of looking at assets because of the society we live in. I too had a messed up way of looking at assets, until I looked at the numbers.

A lot of people believe that their houses, their cars, and their big TVs are all assets. Nothing could be further from the truth. These things are the exact opposite of assets. They're liabilities. *Why?* Because these are things that take money out of your pocket. A car doesn't put any money into your pocket. It costs money to own and it will only depreciate in value.

I'm not saying it's bad to have a car, or that wealthy people don't own cars. However, people on the game plan of wealth realize that their cars or their houses are not assets. They might still buy these things, but they would never refer to them as their "greatest assets" like many mediocre people do.

If it doesn't make you money and/or appreciate in value, it's not an asset.

WHAT IT ACTUALLY IS...

What is an asset then? Well, an asset is something that puts money in your pocket and/or appreciates in value. It's something that makes you wealthier by owning it. I know I just told you that a house is not an asset. But, a house can be an asset if you rent it out because then it functions as a money machine. If you own a house that continuously puts more money in your pocket than it costs to own, then it's an asset. Unfortunately, this is not what the majority of people do with their houses.

> *"I wanna own where I can rent and I wanna rent where I live."* - Grant Cardone

If you buy a house and you rent it out, that's an asset because it's putting money in your pocket. This is real estate investing; one of the greatest ways to build wealth today.

So, to be honest, virtually everything can be an asset and everything can be a liability. It all comes down to whether or not your investment makes money or takes money.

An asset can be a money system, like I talked about in the last chapter. A system that continuously puts more money in your pocket than it costs to own. Examples of this can include:

- A book that keeps making you money.

- A business that makes you more money than it costs to own.

An asset can also be an investment like I talked about in the last chapter. An investment is when you multiply your money by buying something that, eventually, will pay you back more than you invested. The good thing about investments is that, often, once you've invested your money, you'll keep making money forever without doing anything.

Examples of investments include:

- A property you rent out, thus making you more money than it costs to own

- Paper assets that pay you dividends and/or appreciate in value (stocks, bonds, etc.)

Now, there might be a million different kinds of assets out there. What's important to realize, however, is that whether or not something is an asset is extremely simple. **It's an asset if it puts money in your pocket and/or appreciates in value.** If owning the item makes you wealthier, *it's an asset.*

Income is king and the best way to generate scalable passive income is to own assets. Thus, assets are the holy grail of building wealth. For business owners and investors (the ones who are getting extremely wealthy), acquiring assets is the main part of their wealth generation. The more income we generate and the better we handle that income, the wealthier we'll become. Assets are the single best way to do that.

LIABILITIES

So, assets are investments that put money in my pocket? Gee, I wonder what liabilities are then...

Man, I really hope all the 55-year-old conservative people, the "financial experts," and your traditional, conventional aunt won't whoop my ass for saying this. It's just that, the absolute greatest way to explain what liabilities are, is to point at what these people have called their "greatest asset" their entire lives. A great example of a liability is a house.

Liabilities are things that take money out of your pocket, cost money to own, and/or depreciate in value. With a big down payment, a 30-year-mortgage with interests, the new roof, the oven that broke, and all the other things that cost money in a house, it's just the mother of all liabilities. Not to mention all the times you have to mow the lawn, handle your garden, and clean the house.

Buying a home might have been the way to wealth 50 years ago. We're not there anymore, though. Owning a home can be great. However, you should never, ever, ever buy a home as a way to get wealthy. **Buying a home is what you do when you're already wealthy. It's not how you get there.** *Not anymore.*

Okay, I'll stop talking about how buying a home is like digging your own financial grave... for now. The reason I brought it up, though, is to prove my point that people on the game plan of mediocrity are buying liabilities in the belief that they're actually buying assets.

On the game plan of poverty, we buy liabilities knowing that we're buying liabilities and ruining our financial lives. Examples of this can include parties, the new iPhone, an expensive pair of shoes, or a luxury purse. Ask people on this game plan if they're being financially responsible and intelligent, they'll admit that they aren't. They know they're spending their money on liabilities.

On the game plan of mediocrity, however, people actually believe they're buying assets. When they buy that home, they buy that second BMW, and they get that new TV, they actually believe they're getting wealthier. *Why?* Because that's what they've been told by everyone, including the "financial experts." This is such a shame because many of these people actually want to get wealthy. They just don't know that what they're buying is ruining their chances of wealth.

Another crucial thing to realize about liabilities is that, in most people's eyes, they make you look wealthy. Owning two BMWs, a nice home, and the big TV will, in most people's eyes, make you *look* like you're winning the game. You're a champion in the game of money.

So, ironically, most people will actually determine your wealth by the number of liabilities you own. This is the stupidest thing ever because, for this reason, a lot of people spend their money on liabilities to *look* rich instead of buying assets to *be* rich.

This means that, in the pursuit of looking wealthy, most people buy liabilities that make them less wealthy for every month that goes by. **Most people focus on *looking* rich while only a few focus on *getting* rich. The latter are the ones who'll eventually get very wealthy and, ironically, will look a lot richer than everyone else.**

Liabilities are what people on the first two game plans spend their time and money on acquiring, which makes wealth very improbable for them. These liabilities can be everything from a big TV to buying a home.

> *"An asset is something that puts money in my pocket. A liability is something that takes money out of my pocket."* - *Robert Kiyosaki*

FINANCIAL FREEDOM

I'm sure you've heard a lot of people talk about financial freedom. A lot of people talk about it these days because it's a great thing to have. Financial freedom is awesome, and more and more people are starting to realize this. Money isn't everything... but when it comes to the world-class lifestyle, financial freedom is one of the major keys. So, yeah, financial freedom is great.

What is it, though?

You see, a lot of people might talk about this concept. What's funny, however, is that not a lot of people can give this awesome concept a definition. What is financial freedom? I hear a lot of people preach financial freedom but none of them really give it a solid definition.

You see, financial freedom is many things. It's when you have the opportunity to do whatever you want without having money limit you. It's when you aren't forced to work at a job because you generate enough income to live life like you want to.

Here's the definition, though: **Financial freedom is when you can do whatever the fuck you want, whenever you want to.** Well, this is my definition, at least. Honestly, I feel like everyone has their own ideas about what financial freedom means to them. What most people agree on, however, is that it's something along the lines of living life like you want to without being told what to do.

"Yeah man, that's great and all. It's a little weird that you randomly talk about this in a chapter about cash flow, assets, and liabilities, though." Well, this financial freedom stuff is actually super relevant to this chapter. *Why?* Because your financial freedom, even your overall level of wealth, is determined by your income and expenses. Now, what is controlling income and expenses? Well shit, that would have to be assets and liabilities.

So, if you want to achieve financial freedom and be able to do whatever you want to, whenever you want to, without money limiting you, you have to understand the difference between assets and liabilities... and then acquire a ton of assets.

So, yeah, to live the world-class lifestyle, you need financial freedom. To achieve financial freedom, or even wealth, you have to understand this chapter and try implementing this information in your life.

OPM (OTHER PEOPLE'S MONEY)

Alright, so you know you should go out and build, acquire, and/or purchase assets. Good assets aren't cheap, though. If you want to go out there and get yourself a nice 16-unit apartment building, it's going to cost a lot more than what most people have to invest.

This is why it's crucial to learn how to use OPM. You see, a great way to acquire assets is to use other people's money instead of your own. This way, by leveraging other people's money, you can get involved in big investments without already having a fortune.

Because of this, you can quickly make a lot of money, instead of having to wait for your 7% return on your $230 investment to make you wealthy. Remember how we talked about cutting the first part of the compound effect curve off? The best way to do this, without a doubt, is to use other people's money.

"Uuh, yeah, I'm pretty sure using other people's money is unethical and illegal." First of all, nothing in this book is unethical, much less illegal. Second of all, it's not illegal because the person whose money you use will also make money.

Think about someone in your family who owns a home. Maybe your parents do. Now, did they buy that home 100% in full with cash? Chances are they didn't. They used OPM. They didn't use their own money to buy that home, they used someone else's. In this case, the bank's money.

Now, you can actually do the same. But, instead of using other people's money to buy liabilities, you can use their money to buy assets that will put money in your pocket. You can use someone else's money to buy an asset that you might not have been able to afford with your own money. This is very popular in real estate investing. You rarely see an investor buy a property with 100% cash. He buys it with the bank's money.

So, why would people let us use their money to buy assets for ourselves? Well, because we'll pay them back the full amount *plus interest*. This way, they'll make money too. You obviously know about this concept from banks, investors, and private lenders. These people let us use their money and then, in return, we'll pay them back later.

I know I keep bringing up real estate investing, but it really is a great example for how this works. Also, I'm a huge fan of real estate investing and I believe it's one of the best ways to create wealth today. An example of using other people's money to acquire assets is to take a loan out at a bank to purchase a property that you can rent out and make money with.

The idea is to spend a portion of the profits generated to pay back the loan and then enjoy the leftovers. If you buy a property, your tenant should pay more in rent than it costs to maintain the property and to pay back your mortgage + interest.

Here's an example of how a successful real estate investor does it:

1. He takes out a loan at a bank to buy this property.

2. The tenant pays $1,300 for rent every month.

3. The investor gives $900 of those profits back to the bank as he's paying off his mortgage plus interests.

4. It costs $220 a month to maintain the property.

5. He enjoys the $180 monthly profits.

Now, these numbers were just examples that took me three seconds to think of. The numbers out there can be a lot lower and they can be a lot higher. The point, however, is that you wanna buy an asset that will, by generating income, cover the maintenance costs and pay back the loan while still making a profit after all that.

You see, by using the bank's money to invest in a real estate deal, two very awesome things happen:

1. You'll have monthly, passive income that doesn't need you to do anything.

2. Your tenant will, by paying his rent, actually pay for your mortgage. Literally, the tenant will be paying the maintenance cost of your property, he'll pay back your mortgage + interests, and, finally, he'll put money in your pocket. He'll do these wonderful things every single month.

So, not only are you generating a steady, passive income out of thin air by using other people's money, you're also paying more and more off of your mortgage. Well, your tenant is paying off your mortgage. This means that, in addition to the passive income, you'll actually own more and more of a home. Eventually, when your tenant has paid enough of your mortgage, you can sell the house, give the bank its money, and you'll easily be able to make a six or seven figure profit. This is how wealthy people do it.

So, yeah, when people tell you that all debt is bad, you'll want to slap them on the side of their head. **Debt, when leveraged correctly, is one of the greatest tools for creating wealth. Without it, the process can be very slow.**

You can ask almost every wealthy person if they used debt to create their wealth and they'll say yes. They use other people's money to create wealth for themselves. This is not unethical in any way because the person whose money they're using will also make money through interests. This is why banks exist.

When trying to acquire assets, I would definitely recommend using other people's money in addition to investing your own. Especially in the beginning when you have nothing because, again, it's gonna be a very slow process the first 30 years if you start your snowball with only a few hundred bucks. You wanna start with the big assets as soon as you feel like you can control it because, by doing it this way, you'll achieve great financial results a lot faster.

> *"If you can't make sense of a $20,000,000 deal, you can't make sense of a $20,000 deal. If the zeros freak you out, you're in trouble." -Grant Cardone*

You see, it's not harder to handle a $30 million deal than it is to handle a $50,000 deal. So, you might as well play in the league where your efforts, your money, and your time will reward you the most. That league is the big league. Because, I mean, if the amount of work is the same, which it is, then why not jump straight to the big leagues and make a ton of money immediately?

There are two ways to jump straight into the big leagues from having nothing. The first way is to have a wealthy dad who decides to give you a small loan of a million dollars. The second option is to leverage other people's money and put yourself in good debt. This can be from investors or banks.

I hope you now realize that not all debt is bad and that debt, in fact, can be an awesome wealth creation tool if you leverage it the right way. I'm sorry, Dave Ramsey.

BAD DEBT

So, I've been talking about how debt can be a great tool for creating wealth. However, it can also be a great tool for a shitty life full of misery and poverty. You see, there's good debt and that's great. There's also bad debt, though. And, to be honest, that's what most people are getting involved with. They're putting themselves into bad debt, believing they're well on their way to wealth. So, to make sure you don't use bad debt as a way of getting wealthy, let's get clear on what bad debt really is.

Bad debt is debt that takes money out of your pocket. Bad debt is a liability. Examples of this include mortgages on a home that you're paying yourself. It can also be a loan for a new car, phone, TV, couch, or other things that won't make you richer. This way, you'll have to pay off your loan every single month while the item you bought for that money isn't making you any profit at all.

Or even worse, the item you bought, too, takes money out of your pocket. You'll then have acquired *two* liabilities, all in the belief that you're the man and that you're on your way to wealth.

This is really bad debt and it will ruin your chances of financial freedom.

So, yeah, debt is bad when it's a liability. As we all know by now, if it's a liability, then that means it's taking money out of our pockets. **If the investment can't pay off the loan every month and still profit, then it's bad debt.** You lose money by taking on this loan and it's for that reason a liability.

Now, I'm not saying you should never take a loan to purchase that dream car, that nice vacation, or maybe even a home. That's totally up to you. However, don't you ever use this bad debt as a tool for creating wealth. Don't take on bad debt in the belief that it'll make you wealthy. *It won't.*

GOOD DEBT

Good debt is when you take on a loan to invest in something that can pay off the loan while putting money in your pocket. This way, taking on the loan will make you money. Taking this loan and taking on this debt will actually make you wealthier. This is good debt and it's one of the greatest tools when it comes to creating wealth and acquiring assets. **With good debt, you're using other people's money (OPM) to invest in assets that will put money in your pocket and pay off your debt.**

CONCLUSION

Woah. This was a ton of information. Most of it, hopefully, gave you a lot to think about since you've probably been hearing a lot of different things from society. It might all be a lot to grasp and you really shouldn't bum yourself out if there's some of it you don't understand. Especially if you're new to the game of money, entrepreneurship, business, and wealth.

But you know, if you feel like all this is a little too much to handle, that means you've gotten a lot more value out of this book compared to the ones who are thinking, "I already know this."

I know I talked a little about *a lot*. I didn't dive very deep into these concepts. I realize I pretty much just scraped the surface on some of these concepts - in this chapter and in the book in general. It's just that I really can't cover everything about every concept.

You see, society has spoon-fed you so much bullshit and you've been told so many lies. Because of this, there are a lot of things I want you to realize about money and wealth. I want to give you everything you need to get on your way to wealth, freedom, and the world-class lifestyle. Unfortunately, that can't be done in a single book.

So, my idea was to tell you a little about a lot of the parts involved in creating wealth and achieving freedom. Then, you can pick and choose which concepts you want to dive into first. You can then, if you're interested, get help personally from me with that specific concept.

A ton of the stuff I talked about in this book will seem overwhelming as fuck and it might paralyze you a little bit. I don't want that to happen, though. So, I'd love to invite you to the exclusive Cure Mediocrity Facebook group (Facebook.com/groups/CureMediocrity). This group is only for ambitious people with the hunger for wealth, freedom, and the world-class lifestyle.

In this group, we're all on the journey to live the lifestyle we desire. None of us are satisfied with normal, average, or mediocrity. We want the next level and we all realize that the fastest way to do so is to help each other. So, in this group, you'll be a part of a community full of like-minded people who all want to help you achieve your goals and dreams. You'll be a part of a community that will raise your standards and push you to the next level.

Cure Mediocrity is not just a community, though. It's a movement. It's a movement full of young, ambitious people and we are going to change the game. Considering you're still reading this book, I assume you're pretty serious about success and about reaching your potential. So, I would definitely recommend you go join our community. This is, without a doubt, the best way to get started with all this stuff. Who knows, you might be our next success story!

By the way, to anyone who has anything against me promoting this group in my book, fuck off. It's an exclusive, next-level community and I would never, ever, *ever* try to sell you on anything I didn't think was truly a game-changer. I would never promote anything if I didn't believe it had the potential to change your life. Oh, and it's 100% free. Just join the community, man.

[11]

35 DISTINCTIONS

To many people, it might seem like rich people got their money by one single lucky event. The basketball player who signed a $50 million contract. The actor who made a movie and was paid $80 million for the role. Or perhaps it was someone selling an app to Facebook or Google, raking in a cool $45 million.

What people don't understand about these "overnight successes" is that they're all far from being overnight successes. You see, **overnight success doesn't exist.** Even people like Michael Jackson who became successful at age 6 or 7 still didn't get to that success easily. All these people that "suddenly" got really wealthy have all been through a long process before they got to that point.

Every basketball player who signs a big-money contract has worked his ass off every single day for *years*. Finally, he gets rewarded for this tough process and work ethic, and everyone starts calling it an overnight success and everyone talks about how lucky the guy is. What you have to realize is that wealth, freedom, happiness, health, fulfilment, and success in every other area of life, is not an event. It's not about luck or about having it easy.

It's all about your mindset.

Thoughts → Emotions → Actions → Results

Many people hear about taking action toward their dreams and they think they need to change what they're physically doing. In a lot of people's cases, though, the problem is rooted deeper than the action they take. Their lack of success is often not because of their actions, but their mindset. **Lack of success is often rooted deeper than the actions one physically takes. In almost all cases, it's because of one's mindset.**

So, as you can probably imagine, it's a huge advantage to have the right mindset when it comes to money, success, and every other important area of life. In my opinion, it's an absolute necessity. Having a mindset that supports your ambitions and goals is extremely essential. You cannot achieve level 10 results with a level 4 mindset. Unfortunately, this is what many people attempt. Eventually, they all get very disappointed.

So, what's the *right* mindset? How do you know if you have the mindset you need to achieve what you want? Well, look at people who don't have what you want. Don't think like they do. Then, look at people who have what you want. Think like they do.

That brings us to the next question. How do you know how wealthy and successful people think? Well, you do that through years and years of research. Fortunately, for you and me, other people have already done that. There are great books, courses, and training materials out there on how successful people think. You don't have to read or buy all those training materials, however, because I did. At least many of them. I then wrote a book about the best, most valuable things I learned.

This chapter will be about some of the differences that top researchers found between mediocre and wealthy people. These are distinctions that seem to go again when it comes to success or failure in life. It's funny how almost every successful person is thinking, not the same, but very much alike on a lot of areas in life. At the same time, mediocre people share a lot of views and perspectives, too.

So, studying the differences between wealthy people and mediocre people is an incredibly powerful thing to do. Once you've read this chapter, I hope you'll consider thinking more and more like wealthy and successful people do.

BEFORE GOING IN

Before going in I want you to realize 3 very important things:

1. I don't hate people with mediocre mindsets. A lot of my friends and family think this way because almost everyone does. If I were to dislike every person with a mediocre mindset, I'd get really lonely, really fast. Actually, I think the fact that I'm doing everything I can to help people with this mindset means I care about them. If I hated people with this mindset, I'd probably ignore them and do my own thing and not talk about it. I have nothing against people with this mindset. I've just realized that, if we want more than mediocrity, we simply cannot have a mediocre mindset.

2. I refer to people's mindset, views, and perspectives, not their current level of success. You see, I'd say I have a mindset for success and wealth. Yet, I'm still not where I want to be. A lottery winner can have a shitty mindset but still be rich. Eventual-

ly, though, he'll lose it all like almost every lottery winner does. And, eventually, you and I will get very successful like every person with the right mindset does. So, this chapter will not be high income versus average income. It will be powerful, valuable, positive, and effective ways of thinking that will increase your chances of success and wealth versus a limiting, negative, and hindering mindset that pulls you away from your dreams. Not all mediocre people share all these mediocre viewpoints, and the same thing with wealthy people. However, the more of these viewpoints you share with wealthy people, the bigger your chances of wealth and success will be.

3. If you find that you share a lot of the mediocre mindset attributes, don't get discouraged. I remember reading a ton of books on the differences between average and successful people. Every time I shared an opinion or a viewpoint with average people, I felt so discouraged. This is totally the wrong way to look at it. Look, if you find that you may need to change how you look at a few areas of life, that's great. Please realize how awesome it is that you think about these things now, instead of later when it might be too late. So, if you find that you share some of the mediocre viewpoints, don't get discouraged. Be grateful that you've found an opportunity to improve.

1. FITTING IN

Fitting in and being like everyone else. To some people, that's the goal. To others, that would be a nightmare.

You see, most mediocre people have this desire to fit in. It begins when we're like 3-years-old and, for most mediocre people, this desire to fit in never disappears. Because of this, they spend their whole lives trying to do what everyone else is doing. What you must understand, though, is that **you will never get ahead by doing the exact same thing everyone else does.** Just because everyone you know is gonna work at a shitty job for 40 years doesn't mean you have to. Actually, it means you probably shouldn't.

Wealthy people understand that when everybody starts doing something, it's time to do something else. This is why a lot of rich people made a ton of money in pretty much every financial crisis. Because when everyone is selling, it's a great time to buy. If you want to get ahead and really win in life, you have to stop trying to fit in. If you want to live the extraordinary lifestyle, you simply cannot do what everyone else is doing because, you see, everyone is certainly not living the extraordinary lifestyle.

The goal is not to fit in. The goal is to get out as fast as possible and do your own thing. Be *different* - it's the greatest advantage one can have in life.

2. CIRCUMSTANCES

Some people are victims while others make sure they're in control of their circumstances. A lot of mediocre people are victims. We hear it all the time. "My boss is a jerk. They're not paying me enough. I don't have time to care about my health. The only reason I'm not happy is because I'm *unlucky* in life."

Look, even though some of these things might be true, you have to stop complaining and acting like a victim. Instead, *change* things. Your boss is a jerk? Get a new fucking job, man. No one is gonna improve your situation or your circumstances for you.

Wealthy people realize that life is 3% circumstances and 97% perception and attitude. We don't complain and bitch about where we are in life. If we want something, we're gonna reach for it. So, **next time someone complains about his situation without doing anything to change it, tell him to sit the fuck down.** Listen, when things aren't like you want them to be, you can either change it or you can stop focusing on it. Whining and complaining about it is the only thing you should never, ever, ever do.

Here are some wonderful Gary Vaynerchuk quotes on this:

"Complaining is a zero return investment."

"Complaining is very unattractive."

"Stop complaining and stop making excuses. Nobody is listening."

If you're not satisfied with your circumstances, change them. Most people fit their values into their circumstances. I shape my circumstances around my values.

3. HOPE VS. DECISION

Ask some of your friends if they are gonna become wealthy and successful one day. If their answers are along the lines of "I sure hope so," you'll have your answer. They will never become successful or wealthy. At least not if they don't change their mindset right now. Because, like I talked about earlier, **hope is not a plan.**

If, however, your friend said "Absolutely. No doubt about it. I am committed to becoming wealthy and I won't stop until I'm there," that's when you know he's gonna make it. You see, **mediocre people hope for a lot of things. Successful people decide a lot of things.**

"My dream is to be world champion in the UFC and I will be. Guaranteed." - 19-year-old Conor McGregor before all his success.

If you want something, you have to make a damn decision. Don't just hope that it'll happen because, trust me, it won't. If you're committed, however, to doing whatever it takes to get to your destination, that's where the magic happens. If you're not gonna let anything stop you, you'll by definition be unstoppable. This is the point you need to get to. **Don't hope, decide.**

"I always knew I was going to be rich. I don't think I ever doubted it for a second." - Warren Buffett

4. HOPE VS. CONTROL

So, we know that mediocre people use hope as a way to get ahead. Then, what's the opposite of that? The opposite of hope is control. So, if we want to get wealthy and successful, we have to control the variables, instead of merely hoping that the variables will treat us well.

This is why the traditional, mediocre way of doing things sucks. Because all the variables (salary, hours worked, interest on savings, job markets, etc.) are uncontrollable and not scalable. This means that we can't control this plan.

Instead, wealthy people realize they need a plan that they can control. We want to control all the variables. We can do this through businesses, systems, investments, and assets in general.

5. OPPORTUNITIES VS. OBSTACLES

Wealthy people focus on opportunities. What's the end goal? How awesome will this be? Mediocre people focus on the obstacles. How tough is this journey gonna be? How exhausting will this be? To become successful, we have to focus on opportunities, the rewards, instead of the obstacles and the hard work, the price.

Successful people look at the end goal and say, "this reward is worth any journey." Mediocre people look at the journey and say, "no reward is worth this journey."

6. COUNTING SUCCESSES VS. COUNTING FAILURES

This one is *huge.*

Mediocre people measure success by lack of failure and mistakes. "Oh, you only made this number of mistakes? Well done, man." We're taught this early on by the school system. The fewer the mistakes we make, the better we are.

Wealthy people, however, measure success by, well, one's successes. We don't care about how many failures one made. Actually, we often embrace failures and we admire them. People with the wealthy mindset realize that failure and mistakes are stepping stones to success. With failure and mistakes, we'll succeed so much more. **Don't count your failures, count your successes.**

I'd like to prove this with a personal story about my first ski trip. I was with my school and we were all pretty excited because many of us had never skied before. We had a week to learn this ski stuff. My friends and I, unfortunately, all got split up and put into different teams. We wouldn't see each other until 3 or 4 days into the week.

From the first hour I was on skis, I failed so many times, repeatedly smashing my face into the snow. While everyone else on the team would hesitate to try what the instructors told us, I would jump right in and fail. I would try again and again and again. I would fall every time and I'm sure it looked stupid every time, too.

I got better with every single fall, though. And, eventually, only a few days in, I had gotten pretty good at it. I actually learned in a few days what some people take multiple ski trips to learn.

So, it's 3 days into the week and I can finally ski with my friends. One of them comes up to me and says "Dude, I'm so good at this. I've only fallen like 3 or 4 times. How many times did you fall?" I told him I had fallen a good 400-500 times, at least. He then answered with something like, "Well, you're good at so many other things, though." As if having fallen automatically meant I was bad at skiing.

The rest of the week, that guy was still struggling going more than 8-10 miles an hour on the easiest slopes. Meanwhile, I was going way faster down some of the "expert" trails in full control. *What made this difference?* The only difference was my willingness to fail.

This is a great demonstration of how counting mistakes and failures will hinder your successes in life. My friend measured his success on his amount of failures. I measured mine on how well I was doing. The results obviously showed. You see, mistakes and failures are not your enemies; they're tools and they're advantages. Don't avoid them, *use them* to catapult you toward success. This is how wealthy people look at failure and mistakes.

7. Play to Win vs. Play Not to Lose

Imagine this. An entire soccer team decides to stand in their own goal, making it impossible for the opposing team to score. Now, this might be a great strategy for not losing. However, you'll never, ever win this way. Playing all defense will never result in a win, much less domination.

Unfortunately, this is how most mediocre people look at life and money. They're not trying to win... they're trying not to lose. Instead of trying to become great at something and win the game, they settle for a normal, secure job because, this way, they won't lose. They definitely won't win, but the fact that they won't lose is apparently the most important thing to focus on.

Successful people play the game to win. Mediocre people play the game not to lose.

Another crucial difference between mediocre people and wealthy people is that one focuses on expenses while the other focuses on income. Mediocre people will do whatever they can to cut expenses. Wealthy people would rather spend that time generating more income. **Mediocre people focus on expenses. Wealthy people focus on income.** Offense will always destroy defense.

8. Size of Goals

The size of one's goals is one of the most determining factors when it comes to success and failure. The bigger the goals you have, the bigger your results. Grant Cardone, a financial legend, says you should 10x your goals because it will 10x your effort. This is so spot on.

I would much rather get closer to achieving a goal of becoming a billionaire than I would succeed in achieving a goal of earning $5 million.

"I prefer being realistic." Well, who determines what's realistic? Listen, bending a piece of metal, putting humans in it, and then making it fly, that's freaking unrealistic. Yet, the Wright brothers did it. Even though they were told a million times that it couldn't be done.

Listen, set huge goals. Preferably ones you currently can't achieve. You see, when you have a goal that isn't possible to achieve with your current mindset, skills, work ethic, etc., you'll be forced to improve. **Set goals that you currently can't reach. This will force you to grow.**

You see, mediocre people's goals, if they have any, is to get by. They have goals like paying the monthly bills, saving $80, or getting a 2% pay raise every year. Most of them hit those goals, yet they're far from being successful or wealthy.

Failure is not when we aim too high and miss. It's when we aim too low and hit.

Wealthy people reach for the stars. We have goals like feeding 2 million people or changing the world for the better. When we set goals for our finances, we don't have goals like getting a 2% pay raise. We set goals 260 times bigger than everyone else. You should see my list of goals. Now, I don't get scared often, but when I look at my own list of goals... damn. Wealthy people realize that big goals are the way to go.

You can tell a lot about a man's future by the size of his goals and his commitments.

9. ADMIRING SUCCESS VS. HATING ON IT

Jealousy can do a lot to a person. It turns some people into haters. For others, it inspires them to go out and do great things themselves.

Mediocre people, when they see someone who is successful and wealthy, begin to hate. They begin convincing themselves that this guy must be a loser or even a bad person. "Gee, look at that clown in that Ferrari over there. I wonder how many babies he had to kill to get a car like that." This mentality is very popular among mediocre people. This is why every successful person out there will have haters. Because there are small, mediocre minds out there that can't handle their jealousy.

Wealthy people, however, admire success. When we see someone do great, we don't convince ourselves that we don't wanna do great too. Nah, we get inspired and we learn from the person. We then go out and do it ourselves. Eventually, we'll be the one inspiring great minds and offending small, mediocre minds.

Successful people use jealousy as inspiration to do great for themselves. Mediocre people can't handle their jealousy, so they hate.

10. BLESSING WHAT WE WANT VS. RESENTING

The way your mind is conditioned has a lot to say when it comes to making decisions. Often, without you noticing it, your brain is making decisions based on what's right or wrong in your brain's opinion. So, if you continuously condition your brain to hate money, wealth, luxuries, and other cool stuff, you'll actually condition your brain to steer you away from these things.

I know a lot of people who deep down want to be wealthy and have freedom. However, when they see someone with money, they call him or her *greedy*. When they see nice cars, nice houses, or other nice luxuries, they convince themselves that they don't want "stupid, useless" things like that. I have a lot of family and friends that connect having money with awful things like never being there for your children, having bad health, and being a greedy pig.

Obviously, since these people try to convince themselves daily that wealth is a terrible thing, they'll never achieve it. They condition their brains to believe that these things are horrible, thus telling their brains to steer away from it. You might not believe in ideas like the law of attraction but no matter what, there's no denying that conditioning your brain is a very real thing. It's not motivational rah-rah. It's very real and *very* powerful.

When you condition yourself to resent something, you're making sure your brain steers you away from those things. When your brain does whatever it can to steer you away from wealth, freedom, and the world-class lifestyle, good luck achieving it. It won't happen.

When people with the wealthy mindset see something they want, they strengthen that feeling of desire instead of weakening it. When I see a nice car, I'm saying things like "that car is really awesome. I want a car like that. Also, I'm sure the owner is a nice guy with good values. He probably has a lot of good things going for him in life." This way, I strengthen my desire for the car. I'm conditioning my brain to want that car. This way, my brain will steer me in the direction towards these awesome things.

Every second of every day you're conditioning your brain. Be very careful what you condition it to.

11. WEALTH IS UNETHICAL VS. POVERTY IS UNETHICAL

Is being wealthy unethical or is it unethical to be poor or mediocre?

Mediocre people feel that having more money than you need is unethical. This way, you, for some weird reason I've never really understood, take from the poor. Yes, you might be giving millions away to charity. Yes, you might be paying 400 times more taxes than mediocre people do, strengthening society. Yes, you might provide a ton of value for millions of people. Yes, you might be creating hundreds or thousands of jobs. You might believe you're doing great things for the world. However, what you're actually doing by building huge, valuable businesses, is taking food out of homeless people's mouths. Sarcasm might occur.

You see, I had a huge grin on my face while writing that because it's just so ludicrous on so many levels. There's everything wrong with that way of thinking. Yet, this is actually how many people look at rich people. Mediocre people often look at rich people as being the reason for poverty. This is a very bizarre way to look at things, in my opinion.

I agree, there might be some unethical rich people out there, just like there are unethical poor and middle-class people. We have unethical people in every race, every sex, every religion, and all other ways of categorizing people. In every category of people, there will be unethical jerks.

What we have to realize, however, is that the rich are contributing so much more than anyone else. It's people like Bill Gates who donates billions of dollars to charity. How many corporate managers do you know who do that?

Wealthy people are NOT taking money out of poor people's hands and they're definitely not the cause of poverty. It's the exact opposite. Becoming wealthy is an extremely ethical and honorable thing to do. With money, we can contribute so much more to everyone else. We can help our family and friends, society, homeless people, poor countries, etc. How many people making $25,000 a year donate millions every year to charity? No one, because they can't.

Wasting your potential is unethical. Getting wealthy is not.

Wealthy people did not become wealthy by taking from others. They became wealthy by giving a lot more than mediocre people do. Getting wealthy is not only ethical, it's honorable and virtuous.

By the way, I'm not saying that the poor children in Africa are douchebags because they're poor. They don't have the opportunities we have. What I'm saying is that if you have the opportunity to be great and you decide not to, it will influence others in a negative way. Things you would've been able to do for your family, your friends, poor people, and the entire world won't be possible because you decided not to take advantage of the opportunities and the potential you have. That's unethical.

12. CIRCLE OF INFLUENCE

Your circle of influence is one of the most important things when it comes to success and wealth. Your circle of influence is the people you spend a lot of time around. It's the people you share your ideas with. The people you share your dreams and goals with. These people will have a huge impact on your future.

"You are the average of the 5 people you spend the most time with." - Jim Rohn

Mediocre people hang around other mediocre people. They talk about mediocre things and they share their mediocre viewpoints. Because of this, none of them ever expand their viewpoints. They don't grow and they don't evolve because how would they know what to evolve into if they aren't around people who have evolved? This is one of the biggest reasons that mediocre people are mediocre. They spend time with people who pull them back or, at least, doesn't push them forward.

Wealthy people, however, try to find the best possible people to be around. Imagine what your level of success would be if your best friends were Elon Musk, Bill Gates, Grant Cardone, and other highly successful people. You would become successful faster than you could blink.

Now, obviously, your chances of hanging around these people might be a little nonexistent. The idea, however, is extremely powerful. Hang around the best people you possibly can. Find people who have done what you want to do or at least know how to get you where you want to go. This is so powerful and it will make a huge difference in your future success and wealth. Now, if you can't find these people in person, you can read their books, articles, etc. You can watch their interviews and listen to their audiobooks.

Also, you can join communities full of like-minded people. Communities full of people with huge ambitions and the hunger to be great. This is one of the best things you can do if you're serious about success, wealth, freedom, and the world-class lifestyle. When it comes to awesome, free communities with ambitious and like-minded people, I recommend the ones rhyming with "Cure Tediocrity". Those are usually the highest value. We actually have a group called Cure Mediocrity you could join.

Also, don't tell anyone this, but I'm actually working on an exclusive, next-level membership that will change the game for everyone involved. It's not up and running yet but when it is, my God do you wanna be a part of that. Joining projects and communities like these is so freaking powerful.

13. BEING THE SMARTEST PERSON IN THE ROOM

"If you're the smartest person in the room, you're in the wrong room."

This is a quote wealthy people live by. Ideally, you wanna be the dumbest person in the room. This way, you'll learn the most. You see, again, the better people you can be around, the better you'll become. **If you're the smartest person in the room, it means that room won't push you to higher standards. Get out and find a room that will.** Always try to be around people who make your accomplishments look like nothing. This can be very hard on one's self-esteem. Trust me, though, it will catapult you toward success.

Not long ago, I went to a huge business conference called 10X Growth Con hosted by Grant Cardone. Everyone I met was killing the business game in a way I dreamt of doing myself. My self-esteem got shattered with every person I met. Trust me, though, that 3-day event was the most powerful thing that has ever happened in my life. Because of the people I met there, I've raised my standards to whole new levels. I could've never done this without being in an environment where most people were doing so much better than me.

Mediocre people, however, aim to always be the smartest person in the room. If they're not, they'll find a room with lower standards. This way, they'll be the "best" in the room, which many mediocre people like.

We're again back to the fact that **wealthy people want to be around world-class people so they can learn and grow. Mediocre people want to be around losers so they can seem superior.**

14. BEING PROMOTED TO OR SOLD TO

I have a lot of friends who, when they see a salesman, immediately say things like "ugh, a salesman. He's probably gonna try to sell us something." This way of thinking suggests that being sold or promoted to is a bad thing like we're being forced to buy. This is how many mediocre people think. Every time they're being promoted to or sold to, they instantly believe the salesman is only doing so for his own purposes. They're not considering that the offering might be useful to themselves. For some reason, most mediocre people hate being sold to.

Wealthy people see a salesman as someone who brings opportunities. If I'm being sold or promoted to, two things can happen. I can either go away and reject the offering or I can accept the opportunity. None of these things can possibly be bad in any way. I honestly don't get how being offered an opportunity, that you can always say no to, can be bad. As long as the salesman is telling you the truth, how can an opportunity be a bad thing?

And by the way, if you hate being sold to, you should probably run now. You see, I'm without a doubt gonna try to sell you something at some point. This book was sold to you, too. If someone didn't sell you this opportunity, you wouldn't be reading this right now. So yeah, in case you want more of me after reading this book, which I hope you do because I definitely want more of you <3, you should be prepared to one day be sold something to.

Now, I promise you that I will never sell you on something that isn't extremely valuable. I'm not gonna ask you to pay me unless I truly believe my offering is worth at least 10 times more than what you pay. I'm also not gonna spam you, ever. Plus, for every paid offering I promote, I'll be giving away at least 9 awesome free things. So, you can be sure that if I decide to sell you something one day, it will be 100% worth it and you'll be glad I offered you the opportunity.

If you hate being sold to, I have bad news for you. You're getting sold to every single day and you will be forever until the end of time.

15. PROMOTING OR SELLING

Just like mediocre people don't want to be sold or promoted to, they don't want to sell or promote themselves either. Mediocre people have a hard time selling themselves or their skills and values to others. This is very unfortunate because, this way, it can be difficult to get ahead.

Wealthy people, however, become so good that they feel like they have to promote themselves. Wealthy people do not think it's unethical to promote and/or sell something, especially not themselves. We actually think it's unethical not to do because, if we don't, we're actually taking that opportunity away from people.

You have to be ready to go into your boss' office and say "I can do this, this, and this if you, in return, pay me more. I'm extremely valuable and I will continue to get better. I'm worth more." If you don't do this, you'll have a very small chance of being promoted. More importantly, though, you'll actually deny him the opportunity to leverage your more valuable skills. Now *that's* unethical. Selling and promoting is not.

Selling is not unethical. Holding back valuable opportunities is.

16. AVOIDING PROBLEMS VS. SOLVING PROBLEMS

Mediocre people do whatever they can to avoid problems. Wealthy people do whatever they can to solve problems. It's a simple, but very powerful, thought.

Mediocre people avoid problems. Wealthy people solve problems. Strive to be a problem solver.

17. PAID FOR RESULTS VS. PAID FOR TIME

Again, this is an extremely important distinction but there's really not a lot to say about it.

Mediocre people like to get paid by the amount of time they work. Every time they trade their time away, they get paid. The problem with this way of generating income is that there's a limit on your time. You can't start working 32 hours a day because you'll never be able to have that amount of time. Also, even if it was possible, would you really want to spend that much time working? Probably not. So, this way of generating income is very inefficient and not very scalable.

Wealthy people, however, like to get paid for their results. We like to get paid by the amount of value we provide for other people. Because, you see, we can always provide more value for people. We can build better systems, become better at our craft, get creative, or so many other things that will make it possible for us to do more for others. This is why **getting paid for results will always trump getting paid for time.**

18. Net Worth and Passive Income vs. Working Income

How does one measure wealth? How do you know if you're wealthy or not? Well, there's a lot of different ways to determine this.

Mediocre people measure their wealth by looking at their working income, their salary or their wages. They measure their wealth by the amount of money they get paid for trading their time away. And then, of course, their amount of useless liabilities. "Uh yeah man, doing really good. Just got a 3% pay raise and I got my new car. Now if that's not wealth, I don't know what is."

Wealthy people, however, look at two things. We look at net worth, which is all of our assets minus all of our debts. Net worth is everything we own minus everything we owe. The second thing we look at is the amount of income we could put in our pockets every month if we stopped working, also called passive income. Wealthy people focus on net worth and passive income.

19. Educating Ourselves on Money

Education, that's when you go to school and put yourself in a classroom with a teacher, right? Education is something we do to get a degree, *right?*

Well, **saying that school is the same thing as education is like saying tomatoes are the same thing as food. School is one out of a million ways to get educated.** In my opinion, it's one of the least effective ones, but you already know that because I keep talking about it. Also, real education is not something you do to get a piece of paper. Real education is actually something you do to get smarter and learn valuable skills.

Why am I talking about this again? Well, because how you view education determines a lot when it comes to your future success and wealth. Again, I'm not saying that school education is useless. I'm just saying that, to get wealthy, you have to educate yourself on other areas too. You can't just study plant cells and expect to get wealthy. Even if you make a lot of money with a biology job, you'd still not know how to manage that money.

So, wealthy people know how crucial it is to always educate themselves on not only money, but also a lot of other important areas of life. We educate ourselves on money because the better we are at money and the better we understand it, the better we can control and manage it. **Educating yourself on money is not an advantage, it's an absolute necessity.** Because if you don't get educated on money, you'll screw up the next concept...

20. MONEY MANAGEMENT

"The single biggest difference between financial success and financial failure is how well you manage your money." - T. Harv Eker

Money management is the art of controlling exactly where your money comes from, and exactly where it goes. Where your money goes is typically just to taxes and then the rest into your account. At least that's how most people with the mediocre mindset handle money.

Wealthy people, however, purposely split everything they make into a lot of different accounts. Every account has a different purpose and a different goal. Then, we spend or invest those accounts in different ways and at different times. We know exactly where we want our money, and how much. We also know exactly where to spend or save our money, and when to do so.

So, why don't mediocre people handle their money that well? They believe it's not worth it since they don't have enough money. I once asked one of my friend's dad why he didn't manage his money and why he didn't save money to invest. His answer? "I don't have any money."

> *"First you start properly handling the money you have, then you'll have more money to handle." - T. Harv Eker*

When you start handling money, that's when you get more. It's not the other way around. Not having a lot of money is a shitty excuse for not managing your money properly. **Refusing to manage your money because you don't have much is like refusing to eat healthy because you're overweight.** Managing your money well comes first. Having a lot of money comes second. Manage your money well.

21. GRATITUDE

I love this difference. Honestly, I could write an entire chapter about gratitude. It's such an important topic.

Can you be grateful and want more? If you ask many mediocre people, the answer is absolutely not. If you want more, it means you're not grateful for what you have.

As a child, I loved ice cream (as most kids do). When one of my parents or another family member bought an ice cream for me, I would obviously get so happy. What people didn't like about giving me ice cream, though, was that I would ask for more. If I finished an ice cream but wasn't completely full, I would often ask for one more. I didn't get an additional ice cream, but I always tried.

Does this mean I wasn't grateful for the first one? My family thought so. They would say stuff like "you should just be happy about the one you got," or "if one isn't enough, then maybe you shouldn't have had anything at all." I remember thinking that this was very strange. If I wasn't extremely happy with the first one, why would I want another one? If I didn't feel like the first one was awesome, why would I ask for one more? If I hated the ice cream, I wouldn't have asked for another one.

This is how wealthy people think. We actually believe that gratitude is one of the greatest motivators. Also, we believe that working for more is a great way to be grateful for what one already has.

Look, this is how I see it. If I had an ice cream and I want more, it means I was grateful for, and happy about, that ice cream. If I make $50,000 and I want to make another $50,000, it means I'm happy about the first 50k. If I wasn't happy about the first 50k, why would I even work to make 50k again?

I know a lot of people might think this is a weird way of looking at it. But think about it. **Gratitude is the greatest motivator because it will make you want more of what you have.** Hunger for more does not mean you're not grateful, it means you want even more of the good things you have.

22. QUESTIONS

If I asked you what 4 + 4 was, which answer would I receive? I would, hopefully, receive the answer 8 because that's the answer my question was looking for. If I wanted the answer 6, 9, or 13, then I should've asked another question.

So, if you keep asking yourself questions like "why am I not good enough? What can go wrong? Why will I never get rich?" then that's what you will get answers for. You see, your brain is always trying to find the right answers. Your brain works the same way Google does. If you want an answer, that's what your brain will be looking for.

So, let's say you ask yourself "why am I not good enough?" Your brain will ignore everything it knows about how great you are and how many people like you, because that's not what you're asking your brain to find. You're asking it to find reasons for why you're not good enough. This is so dangerous.

When you ask questions like these, two things happen. First, you make a statement that you're not good enough. Second, you're telling your brain to do everything it can to back that statement up.

The questions we ask control our thoughts. If we want positive thoughts, we must ask questions that are looking for positivity.

Wealthy people know this. So, instead of asking negative, useless, or even destructive questions like "why am I never gonna be rich?" we ask questions that empower us. We ask questions like "if I were to help a million people, how would I do it?" or maybe just something like "how can I increase my income by 14% within the next 2 months?"

Your brain might have a lot of negative and disempowering things to say but it doesn't, because you're looking for the answer to these positive questions. By asking questions like these, you will put your brain to work and it will do everything it can to come up with awesome solutions and ideas that will make you wealthy.

23. SAFETY AND OUR COMFORT ZONES

Should you stay in your comfort zone?

Well, most mediocre people would say yes. In one's comfort zone there isn't danger, risk, or opportunity for failure. This is why many people love to stay comfortable. If something scares them, they won't do it. This will limit one's success.

Wealthy people, however, know that they have to get out of their comfort zones to do great things. If something scares them, they know it's often the right move to do. Doing something that scares us, pushes us, or raises our standards is extremely crucial and it's something everyone should do. Especially the ones craving success and wealth.

Mediocre people know there isn't room for failure in their comfort zone, so they stay there. Successful people know there isn't room for opportunity in their comfort zone, so they do their best to get out.

24. COMPETITORS

Competitors. Everyone has them. The question is, who are your competitors and what are you going to do to beat them?

Mediocre people often compete with each other. They know they're doing better than poor people and they ignore rich people because they've "accepted" that they're not gonna get rich. So, they compete with each other. "Oh, you're making $46,000 a year? That's nice. I'm making $48,500, so..." If three of your friends get promoted, you better do so too because else it might look like you're "losing."

When it comes to wealthy people, we definitely compete too. We want to have the best products in the industry and we want to provide the most value for our customers at the best price. Also, we're competing with other investors to get the best deals.

A wealthy person's biggest competitor, however, is themself. We always want to be better than the person we were yesterday. The way I look at it is that I have two competitors in myself. One is someone I must beat every single day, while the other is someone I'm trying my best to reach up to.

The first competitor, the one I must continuously beat, is the guy I was yesterday. I have to always be better than I was the day before. I exercise more intensely, work harder and smarter, read more pages, do more good for other people, etc. every single day.

The second competitor, the guy I'm doing my best to reach, is the highest version of myself. The version of me that reaches 100% of his potential in everything he does. The guy who does the right thing 100% of the time. **I'm never gonna reach the best version of myself because no one ever will. I'm committed to doing my best to get as close as possible, though.** Most wealthy people are.

25. GROWTH VS. KNOW IT ALL

There are two ways to have people admire you. **You can do everything you can to *appear* great or you can do everything you can to *be* great. Choose the second option.**

Most mediocre people are stuck in their viewpoints. To them, it's not about improving and growing, it's about making the best of what you are. So, instead of becoming more, they do what they can to make who they are *look* better.

You can notice this difference in people by looking at how they act in discussions. To mediocre people, a discussion is about proving who's the best or who's the smartest. To wealthy people, a discussion is about educating each other on different ideas, thus both get smarter.

Wealthy people do their best to grow and become the best person they can. They always want to learn, improve, and grow. We realize that this isn't possible if we're stuck in our own beliefs and viewpoints. If we get defensive every time someone is offering us an opportunity to learn and improve, we will never grow. If we never grow, we will lose big time.

So, next time you're having a discussion with someone, ask yourself this: Am I discussing this to learn and/or educate my friend, or am I discussing this to prove I'm better than him at this specific topic?

Always grow and never believe you know it all.

26. WANTING VS. GIVING

Mediocre people are often focused on what other people can do for them. They often think things like "I want to be paid more for my services and my time." This can be at a job or a business, but it can also be with people. It can be with friends or a lover. In almost all areas of life, mediocre people tend to focus on how they can receive. They want want want.

Wealthy people, however, focus on what they can do for others. They try their best to always come up with new ways to improve other people's life. They often ask themselves things like "how can I provide more value for people?" Their focus is not on what they can do for themselves but what they can do for others. The reason for this, is that we realize that we can't receive before we've given.

*"Give value. Give value. Give value. And then ask for busi-
ness." - Gary Vaynerchuk*

*"Try not to become a man of success. Rather become a
man of value." - Albert Einstein*

**Ironically, by focusing on providing value for others, we actual-
ly get rewarded a lot more than if we focused on ourselves.**
Wealthy people know this. So, when we're doing whatever we can
to help others, it's actually not just because we're beautiful angels
sent from heaven. It's because we realize that's the way to win.

27. New Purse vs. Legacy

This is very similar to what I just talked about. The idea is that
mediocre people value a new purse while wealthy people value
legacy.

I'm sure mediocre people want legacy, too. However, it's far
from their focus. The reason a lot of mediocre people go to work
every day is because they have to, or else they wouldn't be able to
survive. What motivates them, however, is the new pair of shoes
they'll be able to afford. The new TV they couldn't buy last
month. This is often why mediocre people work hard, to get more
materialistic pleasures.

Wealthy people, however, focus on things like impact and legacy. We definitely want the nice cars but we want them to be results of us making an impact and building a legacy. Yes, we like
materialistic pleasures, but what really drives us is that we leave
our mark on the world. We don't want to be remembered for just
one generation. We want our grandchildren to tell their grandchildren about us because of what we did.

Again, because our focus is impact and legacy, we get reward-ed so much more than if we were focusing on being able to afford that new purse. We can then buy 200 of those purses and put them in our giant houses, which is awesome. Our focus, however, was impact and legacy.

28. Accepting Defeat vs. "Watch me"

Often, when mediocre people are told that their idea won't work, they go "arh damn, I thought it was a good idea. Well, whatever. Better luck next time I guess," and they give up. Other people telling them that their ideas won't work affect them too much and they eventually decide not to go for it. This is why almost no one ends up achieving their childhood dreams. Because people have told them that it's too "unrealistic," whatever that means.

Wealthy people, however, use doubt as motivation. When peo-ple tell us we can't do something, we just want to do it even more because we wanna prove them wrong. Trust me, there's no better feeling than doing something others told you wasn't possible. Tell Elon Musk that his ideas won't work and he's gonna say "Okay. Thank you. I'm gonna do it anyway, though."

This is the mentality one needs to achieve great things. **Al-ways be open for advice but be very careful what kind of advice you pay attention to.** Don't ever let anyone tell you your dreams aren't realistic, as cliché as that may sound.

Mediocre people accept defeat when someone tells them they can't do something. Successful people spit haters in the face and say, "Watch me."

29. MONEY VS. TIME

What's more valuable, time or money? What I think is not a secret to anyone because I've been talking about it through the entire book. Time is more valuable than money.

Mediocre people like to trade away their time for money. To many mediocre people, time is abundant and they can give away as much of it as possible. Some people with this mindset might even spend hours saving $11 or something like that. To them, money is something one gets in return for time.

To wealthy people, however, time is the goal. Money is just a tool to get the most out of our time. Wealthy people don't trade their time away for money, they actually do the opposite. They trade money away for time. Wealthy people realize that time is the most valuable asset we have.

"Waste your money and you're only out of money, but waste your time and you've lost a part of your life." - Michael LeBoeuf

30. WORKING FOR MONEY VS. MONEY WORKING FOR YOU

This is one of the biggest differences between mediocre people and wealthy people. Mediocre people work for money. Every time they work, they make money. When they don't work, they don't make money.

Now, wealthy people definitely work for money. too. What they do with the money they make, however, is where the difference is. Wealthy people take their hard-earned money and they make it work for them. They find a way to make their money make even more money. This can be done by acquiring assets.

The money you invest in an asset will grow by itself and it will work its hardest to make you, the owner, even more money. This is how wealthy people get wealthy.

> *"The poor and the middle-class work for money. The rich have money work for them."* - Robert Kiyosaki

31. COMPOUND INTEREST

I talked about this in the last chapter, too. Compound interest is extremely powerful when you use it correctly. If you don't use it correctly, however, it'll be pretty useless.

Mediocre people use the compound effect to make money. They invest like $1000 in a savings account and they hope to be millionaires when they retire 40 years later. Unfortunately, when doing it this way, you'll get almost zero profits the first many years. As you saw on the graph I showed in the last chapter, it was actually not until after 40-50 years that the lucrative profits came.

Wealthy people, however, focus on income first. Then, when they have a decent amount of money, they invest. Wealthy people don't use the compound effect to make money, they use it to *multiply* it. The compound effect works best when you have money. You can get money by working for it or you can use OPM (other people's money).

32. SAVING VS EARNING

Mediocre people do whatever they can to save as much as possible of their income. Wealthy people, however, focus more on increasing income. We realize that, when we have a high income, it'll be easier to save and invest. Saving is definitely important, but put your effort into increasing income. Income is king.

33. DEBT

Is debt always bad? Well, if you paid attention in the last chapter, you'd know that **debt is one of the greatest tools for creating wealth.**

Mediocre people think all debt is *bad* debt. They think that debt is something that always takes money out of your pocket. To them, all debt is something that should be avoided. This is what they're told by their relatives, society, and even "experts" like Dave Ramsey and Suze Orman.

Wealthy people, however, use debt as a tool to create wealth. Just like mediocre people, we don't like bad debt. However, we understand the difference between bad debt and good debt. Because of this, we can leverage good debt to make us very, very wealthy.

There's a huge difference between bad debt and good debt. Know the difference, leverage good debt while avoiding bad debt, and you will become very, very wealthy.

34. SCALE, CONTROL, AND TIME

The 3 ingredients. Can it scale? Can we control it? Will you be able to detach your time? These questions are important to think about no matter what you're doing, whether that's a job or a business.

Mediocre people don't think much about these things. When picking their way of generating income, the question is often "how much money will I make the first month?" This is obviously not a very long-term oriented question. Because of this, their income generating solution will often not be very efficient in the long-term.

Wealthy people don't start any projects without first asking themselves these questions. We don't want to go all in on a business and then suddenly find that it's not scalable. So, before going all in on anything, you should make sure to at least consider whether or not your idea has these 3 ingredients. Having these 3 ingredients in your income generating solution will make all the difference later, trust me.

35. "THERE'S MORE TO LIFE THAN MONEY"

This is definitely one of my favorites. I've actually been looking forward to writing about this concept.

"There's more to life than money." Is this true? Are there really other things on this planet that we, as human beings, can find joy in? Absolutely. I'm pretty sure every sane person in the world has other values than just money. This is why mediocre people and wealthy people agree on this one idea. There is a lot more to life than money.

Wealthy people and mediocre people react very differently to this, though.

You see, mediocre people believe there's more to life than money, so they don't do much to get rich. They don't learn about money and they don't create businesses or get in the investing game. Sure, they wouldn't mind being rich but they're not fully committed to becoming rich. Instead of becoming rich, they just want to be comfortable because "there's more to life than money." They're afraid that having too much money might take away some of the other wonderful things life has to offer.

Wealthy people believe there's more to life than money. Their way of looking at this is very different than the way mediocre people do, though. Wealthy people realize that, in order to enjoy all the other wonderful things life has to offer, money simply cannot be a problem. Wealthy people don't believe money is taking other good things away from our lives. Instead, we actually believe money might be the key to all these things, or at least very helpful. With money, we can enjoy all the amazing things life has to offer.

So, when mediocre people tell me I shouldn't go all in on getting rich because there's more to life than money, I simply reply, "Yes, indeed. There's also more to life than working 40 hours a week at a shitty job you hate."

This might be harsh but I hate when people assume that money is the opposite of being with your children. Money is the opposite of being a good person and having friends. Money is the opposite of freedom. These things could not be further from the truth.

With money, you can have freedom. With freedom, you can spend as much time as you'd like with your family and friends. With money and freedom, we have more energy and time to care about our health - mentally and physically. When we care more about our health, we will have more energy and be happier overall. Also, we can travel wherever we want, whenever we want to.

If that's not enjoying the wonderful things life has to offer, then I don't know what is. Sitting in an office doing work you have no emotional connection to, is that what they mean when they say, "there's more to life than money"? That would not make any sense at all.

So, next time someone suggests that having money is the opposite of enjoying what life has to offer, please tell them to sit down and stop talking. There is so much more to life than money. But having money will make it easier for you to enjoy those wonderful things that truly matter.

"Money is not the goal. Money has no value. The value comes from the dreams money helps achieve." - Robert Kiyosaki

CONCLUSION

I just wrote a long ass chapter so I'm gonna make this short. First of all, I want to remind you again that you should not feel discouraged if you agree with many of the mediocre ways of thinking I've listed in this chapter. Honestly, I would be very surprised if you didn't.

How many of the mediocre viewpoints do you think I've had? I've had like 35 of them. We're pretty much all being raised in mediocre environments, so many of us have these beliefs. What's crucial, though, is that we realize the fact that these beliefs ultimately hold us back from our potential. It's important that we get rid of the disempowering beliefs that hold us back and then switch them out with powerful beliefs instead.

Also, I would like to remind you about the 25th concept. The idea that mediocre people are stuck in their beliefs and they defend themselves whenever they're offered an opportunity to learn and grow. Meanwhile, wealthy people want to be the best version they can and they want the best possible results for themselves.

So, when you see something you disagree with, think about this concept. Are you gonna keep your old, disempowering belief and defend yourself or are you gonna be open-minded and actually consider looking at it the way wealthy people do?

I want you to realize that these concepts are not my ideas or opinions. I didn't come up with this stuff. I'm gonna be honest with you, I'm actually pretty new to all this stuff myself. I do not have a ton of experience. This book is not based on my genius ideas that I came up with after 50 years of experience. I wish it was, but it isn't.

These concepts are based on what the most successful and wealthy people have done. It's based upon thousands and thousands of studies. A lot of researchers have spent years upon years to find these things. Wealthy and successful people have been studied for hundreds of years.

Look at it this way. The chef did not catch the fish, he didn't grow the potatoes, and he certainly didn't invent vegetables or meat. What he's doing is simply taking a lot of great stuff that others have created, and then he creates something valuable out of that. He throws away everything he doesn't want and he adds what he thinks would be great. Eventually, he'll end up with a great meal.

I'm the freaking chef.

I'm taking 300 books from here and 47 studies from over there, and then I combine that with tons of valuable research from all over the world. I then remove everything that isn't extremely valuable, powerful, and life-changing. I then add my own personal spice, which can be a unique perspective, an opinion, or maybe just a new way to explain an old concept.

Eventually, I'll have crafted the best meal I possibly can. I hope you're getting that this book is the meal.

I've looked at tons and tons of ingredients just to throw out like 96% of it because it was crap. Because of this, by reading this book, you'll save so much time and energy.

The concepts you're learning about in this chapter, and in the book in general, were not created by me. It's something the most successful people on earth created. I just put it all together and do my best to explain it in an understandable way.

So, if you've been sharing some of the mediocre viewpoints in this chapter, don't get discouraged. However, you should also not ignore it. If there's something you don't agree with, don't just say "arh well, what does it matter if I don't agree with this one concept?"

Instead, I challenge you to really be open-minded and look at it from another point of view. I challenge you to not get stuck in your old patterns and beliefs. This is crucial while reading this book and it's crucial in every other area of your life. So, when someone offers you an opportunity to look at things in a different, more empowering way, don't get offended and start defending yourself or justifying your situation. Instead, seek to understand, to learn, and to grow.

Fuck, I didn't make this conclusion short at all.

PART 4:
CURING PERSONAL
MEDIOCRITY

"Our outer world will always be a reflection of our inner world. Our level of success is always going to parallel our level of personal development. Until we dedicate time each day to developing ourselves into the person we need to be to create the life we want, success is always going to be a struggle to attain." - Hal Elrod

Like many of you, I'm a huge fan of tangible and concrete things. I like numbers and facts. I like systems and rules. I like concrete advice on step-by-step making x amount of money and achieving x amount of success. I like when things are simple and the step-by-step plan is laid out for me.

There's one thing we can't get around, though, no matter how advanced our systems or plans might be. The idea that our outer world is a reflection of our inner world. The idea that the more we grow as people, the more success and wealth we'll be able to attain. You have to be a person capable of success and wealth *before* you can achieve it.

I know a lot of people who couldn't care less about personal development. That's a damn shame because this will limit their success.

You see, if the business idea isn't the greatest, you can come up with something new or you can improve it. If the real estate deal isn't as profitable as you'd hoped it would be, you can always find another deal. You can pick and choose between almost every asset on the planet. If something isn't working, either get a new one or change it so that it works.

You yourself, however, *cannot* be changed. You can't wake up one day and decide "mmh, life as me sucks. I'm gonna be Dan Bilzerian instead." This isn't possible. So, we have to "settle" for the next best thing, which is to *improve* ourselves. If we want to improve our lives, we have to improve ourselves first. The only way to truly improve oneself is to learn and grow.

Money strategies, business systems, and proper investing are all great, and we know how obsessed I am regarding these topics. However, we'll never be able to leverage these things properly if we don't first develop ourselves.

This is why you could give the most amazing money advice to 200 people and only a few of them would actually become wealthy. *Why?* Because they haven't worked on themselves enough to be able to handle amazing money advice.

If you want to get wealthy, get in great shape, and be happy, **you have to work on yourself before you work on specific methods or techniques. Personal development is the first step of every success.**

[12]

PAIN & PLEASURE

Why are some people super overweight while others are in great shape? Why do some people smoke 30 cigarettes a day while others have never smoked in their lives? Why do we decide to do what we decide to do? What are the reasons behind the decisions we make?

Pain and Pleasure. **Pain and pleasure are behind every single decision you've ever made and ever will make.**

> *"The secret of success is learning how to use pain and pleasure instead of having pain and pleasure use you. If you do that, you're in control of your life. If you don't, life controls you." - Tony Robbins*

Unfortunately, very few people realize how crucial pain and pleasure really are. Even fewer know how to control pain and pleasure, and almost no one knows how to use these incredible tools to achieve success and wealth. The ones who do, however, are the ones we all look up to.

WHAT IS IT?

Using pain and pleasure as tools to achieve success is incredibly powerful. What do I mean by "using pain and pleasure as tools," though?

Well, pain and pleasure are the factors behind every decision we make. With every decision we have to make, our brain tries to estimate how much pain and how much pleasure our choice will ultimately provide.

If the specific activity that we want to engage in provides more pleasure than it provides pain, we will make the decision to do that activity. If, however, the activity produces more pain than it produces pleasure, we'll hesitate.

Let's look at why some people are unhealthy while others are not. The reason for this difference lies in how much pain and pleasure the person connects to being healthy.

If a person connects more pleasure than pain to being healthy, that person will without a doubt be healthy. Same thing on the other side. If a person connects more pain to being healthy than he connects pleasure, he'll stay unhealthy. He might give great health a shot for a few days... but eventually, he'll fall back into unhealthy habits.

This is incredibly powerful. If we can control how much pleasure and how much pain we link to doing a specific activity, then we can control whether or not we'll do it. By controlling pain and pleasure, we control all of the decisions and all of the actions we take. By controlling our actions and our decisions, we control our results. Control our results, and we control our lives.

Our brain is just guessing when it estimates how much pain and pleasure a specific activity will produce. Our brain looks at everything it feels about this activity and it then makes an estimate based on that. So, our brain is actually not making decisions based on facts. It's making decisions based on guesses, feelings, and past experiences.

So, if you can't get yourself out of bed early in the morning to run, it's because you link more pain to it than you link pleasure. The good thing about this is that you can actually control pain and pleasure. You can control how much of each you link to running in the morning, thus controlling whether or not you'll do it. By controlling pain and pleasure, you can actually make yourself go from hating to run in the morning to always wanting to do it.

THE GREATEST TOOLS

So, why do some people link a ton of pain to being healthy while others link pleasure? Because when we estimate whether or not something will be more pleasurable than painful, we calculate it by looking at all the negative things and all the positive things.

To explain this, let's look at numbers because I like numbers. Everything above zero is pleasurable and everything below zero is painful. So, if the specific activity gets more than zero points, you'll engage in that activity, e.g. run in the morning. Then, what you do is you take all your references, or your reasons, for why it's pleasurable or painful and you add them together.

Here's an example:

It's exhausting (let's say that's -3 points) and it's cold in the morning (-2). However, I get healthier and I feel great afterwards (+6). In this example, you link more pleasure to running than you link pain. You'll engage in this activity.

By the way, the amount of weight each reason or argument has is determined by the emotional intensity you have regarding that reason. The fact that your running shoes are an ugly color probably doesn't have a lot of weight because it doesn't produce enough emotional intensity. However, if your reason for not running was because you were afraid of being embarrassed in front of people, that would produce a lot more emotional intensity.

So, we estimate whether or not the activity will be more pleasurable than painful by adding up all our arguments for both sides. Here's the interesting thing, though. **We all have different arguments and reasons for why something is pleasurable or painful.**

Ask a very overweight person why she isn't in shape and her answer will probably be something like this: "And give up all my favorite foods? And exhaust myself by exercising every day? I would do all these painful things *for what?* To look a little sexier in a swimsuit? No thanks." As you can see, this person links a lot more pain to being healthy than she links pleasure.

Ask me, however, and I would say something like this: "Be in great shape, be a lot more confident, have tons of energy, live longer, and be overall happier? Yes, thank you. All I have to do is exercise, which is fun, and not eat shitty foods. No problem."

As you can see, I obviously link a lot more pleasure to being healthy than I link pain. Because of this, it's not a problem for me to live a healthier lifestyle. I'm actually excited about being healthy because I know how many wonderful and pleasurable things I achieve by being healthy.

So, if we link more pain to something than we link pleasure, we're basically screwed, *right?* Not at all. Because we can actually manipulate these reasons. We can add reasons that support our morning run and we can decrease or eliminate reasons that tell us it's painful. By doing this, we can go from hating to do something to being super excited about it.

We can always add pleasure to a specific event or activity and we can always eliminate pain.

BELIEFS

As with many other topics in this book, I could probably write an entire book about beliefs. **Our beliefs, or thoughts, determine how we feel about something. How we feel about something determines how we act, and how we act determines our outcome.**

So, if you believe that being healthy is more painful than it is pleasurable, you simply won't engage in healthier activities. But, to change our beliefs, we have to dig a little deeper. Like I talked about earlier, we have to manipulate the reasons, or references, for our beliefs before we can change anything. So, to change our belief about being healthy, we must increase and/or add positive references and we must decrease or eliminate negative ones.

References are the reasons or arguments for a specific belief. Tony Robbins describes it by saying that a belief is the tabletop while references are the legs. So, if we remove the legs, the belief will become wobbly and less certain. If we add or strengthen the legs, we strengthen that belief.

So, the way to manipulate your beliefs is to imagine you have two tabletops. One is the belief that being healthy is painful and one is the belief that being healthy is pleasurable. What you'll want to do is to then strengthen the belief you want and weaken the one you don't want.

QUESTIONS

One of the greatest ways to do this is through asking questions. Like I talked about earlier, **the answer you get is determined by the question you ask.** So, if you want answers that make you believe a certain thing, you have to ask questions accordingly.

Here are two examples of questions that will strengthen the belief that being healthy is pleasurable and decrease the belief that being healthy is painful:

- *What are 10 great things about being healthy?*

- *What are 10 bad things that will happen if I don't become healthy?*

Your brain will automatically come up with answers to these questions. You can then use the answers from these questions to ask more questions, controlling your beliefs even further.

So, let's say one of your answers to the first question was, "I would definitely be more confident." You can then ask questions like, "what are three great things that would happen if I became more confident?" Your answers could look something like this:

- *I would take this confidence to other areas of my life and become overall happier.*

- *I would wanna be more social and meet new people.*

- *I wouldn't be as shy because I would now feel like I was good enough.*

You can then continue by asking, "what would happen if I met more people and became more social? What would happen if I became overall happier?" You can continue to strengthen your desire to get healthy more and more by continuously asking questions. Every time you ask some of these questions, you would strengthen the belief that being healthy is pleasurable.

You can then do the same thing with the belief that being healthy is painful. Ask questions until that belief becomes weaker and weaker. Here's an example:

"What will happen if I don't become healthy?"

- *I won't be as confident.*

- *I'll live a shorter life.*

- *I will not have the energy to be fully there with my friends or family.*

- *I won't be able to give my all in the activities I engage in.*

You can then continue by asking questions like, "What would happen if I didn't have the energy to give my all and to fully be there for my friends and family?" You can keep asking questions until you've made not being healthy seem as painful as possible.

Eventually, you'll find being healthy a lot more pleasurable than painful.

As you can imagine, when you have hundreds of reasons for why being healthy is pleasurable and you have hundreds of reasons for why not being healthy is painful, you'll have no problems focusing on your health. You'll most likely be super excited about it and you will even enjoy it.

This is, by the way, why you see some people who are super overweight for 20+ years and then, one day, they just decide they've had enough. They begin focusing on their health and they get in great shape.

What happened? Well, that day their number went above zero. They suddenly linked more pleasure to being healthy than they linked pain. This can happen because they start thinking about the benefits of being healthy. It can also happen because a doctor tells them that if they don't become healthy, they won't be able to have children.

So, whether or not we want to do something is rooted in our beliefs. Is it more pleasurable than it is painful? Whether or not we believe it is lies in our references. The good thing is that we can manipulate these references by asking the right questions.

HAVE A BIG "WHY"

It's a little weird that I decided to write this chapter in a book about business and wealth, isn't it? Does pain and pleasure have anything to do with getting wealthy and achieving success?

Actually, pain and pleasure have *everything* to do with wealth and success. Creating wealth and achieving success is about making a ton of difficult decisions. **Every decision you make will either lead you away from your dreams or push you towards them. Every decision counts.**

If pain and pleasure determine your decisions and your decisions determine your future success, then pain and pleasure must obviously have a lot to say. So, if you want to control your decisions, you have to control pain and pleasure instead of letting them control you.

The point I'm really trying to make with this chapter, though, is that you need a big fucking *why*. You need a giant, *meaningful* why. Why do you want to be in great shape? Why do you want to get wealthy? And, more importantly, why do you want to be the best person you possibly can? Why do you want to give 100% in everything you do?

If your answer is "I don't know," then your first job, before you do anything else, is to find one or more whys. Find a lot of reasons for why you want to achieve your specific goals.

Becoming successful in any area of life takes a shit load of energy, time, work, money, and other resources. If you don't have a strong why to pull you through when things get tough, you'll give up. I promise.

Getting wealthy, getting in great shape, and becoming successful is extremely simple. However, it's the furthest thing from easy. It's gonna take a ton of work and you're gonna have to make sacrifices. Without a strong why, you will not get through it.

I'm sure you've heard about this concept before. Everyone talks about it. Trust me, though, there's a reason for that. **A strong why is the starting point for all great achievement.**

It's not motivational rah-rah. It's psychology.

If we think something will provide more pleasure than it will pain, then we can better handle the pain. If, however, we keep going through pain and adversity and we don't believe the pleasure will be worth it, we will quit. Guaranteed.

The stronger the why, the more shit you can go through and still keep going.

CHAPTER BULLET POINTS:

- Pain and pleasure are behind every decision we make because they control how we feel about something. And how we feel about something ultimately determines our actions.

- Behind every belief are references. We can manipulate these references, thus manipulating our beliefs. An effective way of doing this is through asking questions.

- Everyone has different beliefs and everyone has different arguments and references for why something may be pleasurable or painful.

- **A huge, meaningful why is the first step of all achievement.** The bigger the why, the more effort you'll put in and the more sacrifices you will be able to make. The bigger the pleasurable reward, the more pain you can go through without giving up.

[13]

RAISE YOUR STANDARDS

Success and wealth do not come from a few big events. As I talked about earlier, it's the small things we consistently do that really matter. It's the entire process that matters. **It's not the big things we do 3% of the time that shape our destiny. It's the small things we do 100% of the time.**

If the things we consistently do aren't pushing us toward our dreams and goals, we have a gigantic problem. The small things we do consistently determine all our outcomes. So, we better make sure these small, consistent things are as effective and as efficient as possible.

We need to make sure that the things we consistently do are as congruent with our goals and dreams as possible. If we want to get in great shape but we consistently eat cheesecake at night, we're probably gonna have to wait a long time to see that six pack, even though we might go for a run once in a while.

We have to make the right decisions as often as possible. We have to consistently make the decisions that push us toward our vision for the future. So, what we have to do is raise our standards. We have to raise our standards and make it a *must* to consistently do what our goals and dreams require us to do.

What we consistently do means everything in terms of future outcomes and results. So, by raising our standards regarding these small things we do consistently, we make sure we always make the decisions that push us toward our dreams instead of away from them.

Because, you see, everyone has different standards. What some people have to put in a lot of effort to do, some people do without even thinking about it. What some people might be super proud of, some people would feel is easy and maybe even below them. What some people fight themselves to do, some people can't not do because it's a must.

"Sometimes... The issue is simply that their ceiling is your floor." - Unknown

I remember when I had such a hard time making myself work out. I remember not being able to get myself out of bed in the morning to go for my run. I remember when I had a tough time being productive and getting work done. Instead, I would play videogames or watch useless YouTube videos.

I've raised my standards, though.

Today, I have to run in the morning. If I don't, it doesn't feel right. It has become a must for me. Same thing with being productive instead of wasting my time. Today, I hate wasting my time on useless things and I don't feel right if I binge watch YouTube instead of doing something useful.

You see, I've raised my standards. What I once had a hard time making myself do is now a *must* that you couldn't pay me *not* to do. What was once my ceiling is now my floor.

At the moment, I'm working on making it a standard to work out in the evenings too. So, cardio in the morning and weightlifting in the evening. This is a little new for me so I still have to fight myself a little bit about that evening workout. I'm raising my standards, though. Eventually, my evening workout will become a standard and it, too, will be a must in my life.

Our standards make the decision for us. When we have a standard about doing something, we don't have to ask ourselves whether or not we should do it. We just do it. So, with the right standards, we can consistently make the right decisions that push us toward our dreams and goals. With high standards, we'll make the decisions our goals require us to make. **Raising one's standards is one of the most powerful things one can do.**

Remember, our future success is determined by the many small, consistent decisions we continuously make. We have to make the right decisions as often as possible and the best way to do that is to raise our standards.

We get praised in public for all the small things we consistently do in private.

The standards we hold ourselves to will determine everything in terms of future success or failure.

WILLPOWER

Many people think willpower is the key to extraordinary results.

It's not.

When you look at someone who's able to stay in great shape, make the right choices financially, always treat people right, and always make the difficult choices in life, it's not because of will-power. This would not be possible. At least not for long. Eventually, she would burn out. Also, she would not be happy.

If you don't have high standards for yourself, it's not because of lack of willpower. Many people believe it is, which is a shame because it's limiting their capabilities.

When I ask my mom why she isn't exercising or why she's smoking, her answer is always "I have a spine like an earthworm," which in Danish is a way of saying someone has no willpower.

Unfortunately, most people don't have a lot of willpower. Most people would rather pick the easy choice instead of the difficult one. Even though we might make the right decision once in a while, it's almost impossible to always do if we're relying on pure willpower.

I'm gonna let you in on a little secret right here. I, too, have a spine like an earthworm. I have zero willpower. Nothing. Nada. If I have to choose between doing the easy thing and the difficult thing, you can count on me picking the easy choice. Sometimes, I can make the tough decisions a few times... but it won't last.

So, *am I screwed?* Should I forget all my dreams about wealth and success?

Fuck no. Willpower is not the key, and lack of willpower is not detrimental. Almost no one can keep going and keep making the right decisions while relying on pure willpower. **Willpower is not the key to high standards and it's certainly not the key to achievement and success. Habit is.** More on habits later.

You see, willpower is like a muscle. By using your willpower, we actually fatigue and exhaust it. Another example can be to look at our willpower like a tank. The more we use, the less we'll have for the rest of the day. Our willpower replenishes itself when we let it rest.

Back in 1996, a guy named Roy Baumeister proved this with a seemingly silly experiment. Baumeister and his team kept 67 participants in a room that smelled of freshly baked chocolate cookies. They even showed the participants a lot of different delicious chocolate-flavored confections.

All the participants salivated at the thought of these delicious chocolate-flavored sweets. However, only half of the participants were allowed to eat the chocolate cookies. The other half were allowed to smell and look at the chocolates, but were not allowed to eat them. Instead, they were asked to eat radishes instead, which they weren't happy about.

They were then handed a completely unrelated exercise, a persistence-testing puzzle. The differences between the two groups were very noticeable and undeniable. Those who ate radishes made far fewer attempts and devoted less than half the time solving the puzzle compared to the chocolate-eating participants. They even added a third group that had nothing to do with the chocolates or the radishes. This group also performed way better than the radish-eating group.

In other words, the group who had to resist the sweets and force themselves to eat pungent vegetables could not find the will to give their all in another completely unrelated task. The two tasks had nothing to do with each other, yet the radish-eating group, who had already used their willpower, had much less to give on the second task. They had exhausted their willpower.

This is what *The Atlantic* had to say about this experiment:

In the psychology world, the key finding of this seemingly silly study was a breakthrough: self-control is a general strength that's used across different sorts of tasks -- and it could be depleted. This proved that self-regulation is not a skill to be mastered or a rote function that can be performed with little consequence. It's like using a muscle: After exercising it, it loses its strength, gets fatigued, and becomes ineffectual, at least in the short-term.

So, self-control, the ability to make decisions based on logic and not emotions, is something that can be depleted. It's like a muscle. While we can definitely strengthen our willpower over time, which is useful, we shouldn't rely on willpower because it *will* be depleted. No matter how strong you are, you won't be able to stay in a planche position 24 hours a day, every day.

So, if we want to get in great shape, handle our money properly instead of spending it on crap, become successful, and overall always make the right decisions, we can't solely rely on willpower. **Trying to make the right decisions 100% of the time by using only willpower is like staying in a planche position 24 hours of the day, every day. Even if it was possible, it would suck. Instead, we must rely on habits and rituals.**

I remember trying this for myself. I wanted to exercise for hours every day while eating only healthy foods. I wanted to read multiple books a week and I wanted to work 16-18 hours a day. I wanted to be some kind of superhuman.

I failed.

I wasn't able to hold these standards up for very long. I failed and I got pissed and frustrated. I was so disappointed with myself. I had seen so many successful people live like this. Why couldn't I do it too? Were my desired standards too high?

My standards were far from too high. The standards we set for ourselves can never be too high. The problem wasn't that my standards were too high. The problem was that I tried to do all these things by using willpower. I was fighting myself with every decision I made, and I expected to win 100% of the fights.

Trust me: you do not want to rely on willpower and always have to force yourself to live up to your standards.

Raising one's standards solely by using willpower is not the way to do it. You will always have to fight yourself with every decision you make. This will drain your energy and it will make life suck.

Your willpower tank will be depleted. So, if you rely on willpower, you will be pretty damn screwed once you've exhausted all of it. This is why so many people try to lose weight and then four days later they cheat on their diets and eat shitty foods again. It's because they tried to raise their standards by using only willpower.

So, if willpower isn't the way to have high standards, *what is?*

HABITS

The greatest way to raise one's standards is to create good habits and eliminate bad ones.

As I said earlier, I do not have a lot of willpower. If I were to wake up and ask myself whether or not I should go for a run, I would stay in bed every single time. I do not have a lot of willpower so when I have to make decisions like that, I take the easy way out, which I'm sure most people do.

Then, how come I run every single day? Well, because it's an automatic thing for me. It's something I do without even thinking about it. I could wake up one day and decide not to run, but I would already be in my running shoes and I'd be in the process of putting on my favorite music.

I have no willpower and if I have to make a tough decision, I'll often pick the easy choice. However, by making my morning run a habit, I don't have to make any decisions. It's not a decision, it's just something I do. When something's a habit, we don't have to think about whether or not we should do it. We just do it.

Brushing your teeth has, hopefully, become a habit for you. Am I right to assume that you don't have to fight yourself every time you have to brush your teeth? You probably don't even think about it. It's just something you do as a part of your daily routine.

Imagine if you could do this with the right health choices. Imagine if you had a habit of working hard. What about a habit about handling your money properly? What about being a great person and making others happy? All these things can be turned into habits.

Once something is a habit, it's a part of you. It's a part of you and your standards. So, as you can imagine, it's incredibly powerful to be full of good habits and have as few bad ones as possible.

Once something is a habit, it will actually often be difficult not to do. I mean, when I have some kind of habit, it feels like there's something wrong with the world if I don't do it. If I skip my routines one day, it feels wrong.

This is the point you want to get to with *every* positive habit.

Can you imagine how much you could achieve if you had an entire arsenal of powerful habits? Success and wealth are not about the few big things you do 3% of the time. It's about the small, consistent things you do 100% of the time. It's about our habits and rituals.

Here are some great quotes for you to enjoy:

"We are what we repeatedly do. Excellence, then, is not an act but a habit." - Aristotle

"Successful people are simply those with successful habits." - Brian Tracy

"You'll never change your life until you change something you do daily. The secret of your success is found in your daily routine." - John C. Maxwell

So, to really raise your standards in a way that's sustainable and that will work long-term, you have to start with your habits. Create powerful habits that make you make the right decisions. **Create habits that continuously push you toward your vision.**

Now, I've hopefully convinced you that creating powerful habits is the way to go. So, *how do we create these habits?*

Well, there's really only one way to do it and that is... survive. Survive until it's a habit. Let's say you want to make a habit of reading 15 pages of a book every day. To make this a habit that will stick, you have to push yourself to do it continuously until it's a habit. This can take between 15 to 70 days, determined by the habit.

So, how do we keep doing this activity over and over again until it's a habit? How do we persist? How do we survive until the activity becomes automatic?

By using willpower.

COMBINE THEM

"Willpower? But I thought you said relying on willpower was a bad idea?..."

So, is willpower totally useless? *Absolutely not.* It all depends on how we use it.

You see, relying completely on willpower is useless and it's stupid. If we rely on willpower, we'll be screwed because our willpower will be depleted, and then what do we do? If we want to perform better and have higher standards in any area of life, we must not rely on willpower.

Again, the power of willpower depends on how we use it. Since it can be depleted, we have to use it wisely. We have to get the most out of it. The goal is not to use more and more willpower. The goal is to get better results while using less willpower.

"It can entail a measure of working hard, but working hard is never the goal. The goal of making a fuel-efficient car is never to figure out how to put tons of gas into it. It's how to put less gas into it and go more miles per gallon." - Tai Lopez

Now, I realize Tai was talking about hard work and not willpower. However, the quote works perfectly with willpower, too.

The goal is to use as little willpower as possible while getting the best results as possible.

A crucial thing to realize is that once something is a habit, it requires no willpower. When we've gotten used to exercising, we don't have to use any willpower to do it because it's a habit.

So, what we want to do is to use the willpower we have to create powerful habits. Instead of spreading our willpower thin by using it to give our all in 47 different areas, **we have to focus our willpower on one specific action until it's a habit. We can then focus on creating a new habit.**

Then, when we've focused our willpower on creating a specific habit, we can create a new one. We can do this continuously and we'll keep developing ourselves. By using willpower to create habits, we can raise our standards for the long-term.

So, instead of using willpower to make you perform, use your willpower to create habits and then let your habits make you perform. By raising our standards this way, we **rely on habits instead of willpower and use willpower as a tool to create habits**, which is extremely powerful.

We can then keep raising our standards by improving or adding positive habits into our lives. We'll become developed people capable of achieving great things.

ALWAYS IMPROVE, GROW, AND RAISE YOUR STANDARDS

Continuous learning is the most crucial thing to do if you want to succeed in life. You don't see any successful people who don't learn every single day. It doesn't have to be much, but you have got to learn and improve on a daily basis.

An extremely powerful thing to do is to commit to always being better than you were the day before. To always be better than yesterday. I strongly suggest you make this commitment. Every successful person has.

Did you ever play one of those racing games where you would compete against your previous performance? This is literally how I live my life. Every day I try to perform better than yesterday. It doesn't have to be much, though.

> *"If you can't fly, then run. If you can't run, then walk. If you can't walk, then crawl. But whatever you do, you have to keep moving forward." Martin Luther King Jr.*

It doesn't have to be huge improvements but seek to always be better than yesterday, even if it's just a little bit. I know it might seem useless in the moment, but imagine improving 1% every day for a year. You would then be 365% better than you were the year before. In the long-term, this makes a *huge* difference.

And that's without introducing the compound effect. With the compound effect, if we improve 1% every day for an entire year, we'll actually be a lot more than 365% better. Improving just 1% every day is incredibly powerful.

Every night, when I lay in my bed, I consider all the things that could've been better and all the great things that happened that day. What usually gives me the greatest feeling of accomplishment and fulfillment is when I've grown. It's when I've somehow gotten better than when I went to bed the day before.

"Progress equals happiness." - Tony Robbins

Progress, *the development of an individual or society in a direction considered more beneficial than and superior to the previous level,* is what makes us happy. This is, by the way, why so many people get depressed. Because they're not growing and moving forward.

I've experienced this first hand. At times where I move forward with speed and I grow, learn, and improve myself while pursuing big goals, I'm incredibly happy. Then, at times where I feel stuck, that's when I get down and lose my excitement about life.

Growing, improving, and learning is highly recommended. I've seen how it transforms people emotionally. When we transform like this emotionally, we will automatically transform our physical, mental, and financial lives, too.

Sometimes, it can be a little difficult to notice when we've grown, though. This is why we have to consciously look for things we've improved at. A great way of making sure you keep improving is to think about it at night when you're in bed.

Try to find at least five things you've learned or areas you've improved in your life. If you ran, you can put your health on that list. If you read something useful about SEO today, then you can put marketing on that list.

Again, it doesn't have to be huge things. It can be super small things. Maybe you improved your morning routine or something like that. As long as you're improving and growing.

So, this is my challenge to you. Every night, for the next seven, days I want you to find at least three things you've gotten better at or have improved at. I'm sure this will become a habit because it will empower you so much that you'll want to keep doing it.

Remember, it doesn't have to be huge things but we've got to always keep growing, learning and improving.

CHAPTER BULLET POINTS:

- The small things we do 100% of the time means everything when it comes to success and wealth. We have to make it a *must* to consistently do what our dreams and goals require us to do.

- Our standards determine our decisions. We must raise our standards and demand greatness from everything in our lives.

- Willpower is not the key for always making the tough decisions. If you rely on willpower to make the right decision 100% of the time, you'll fail. Willpower is like a muscle and so we can't use it 100% of the time. That's like using the same muscle for 24 hours a day, every day. Even if it was possible, it would suck.

- Instead of relying on willpower, we must rely on habits and rituals. When something is habit, we don't have to fight ourselves to do it. We just do it. In fact, it might feel unnatural *not* to do that specific activity. We must create powerful habits that make it easy for us to continuously make the right decisions and take action toward our visions and goals.

- We create these habits by forcing ourselves, through willpower, to do the activity over and over again until it becomes habit. Instead of spreading our willpower thin, we must focus it on creating one habit at a time until that habit is a part of us. We can then proceed to create a new habit.

- Always learn, improve, and grow. And *always* be better than yesterday.

THE BEGINNING

Why is this part called *The Beginning*? Shouldn't it be called "the end" like other authors call the last part of their books? Well, I don't think so. You see, you've been reading this entire book, which is incredible! Kudos to you.

However, as I talked about throughout the book, knowledge is only *potential* power. Information doesn't help anyone if we don't use it and implement it in our lives.

So, it is now time to implement the information, take action, steer yourself in the direction you want to go, and chase your vision. It's time for you to attack your dreams and go create your world-class lifestyle. To me, that's not the end. That's the beginning.

What To Do Now

To give you something to get started on, I would like to lay out the overall steps you can take to start creating wealth, achieving freedom, and living the world-class lifestyle. With these steps, you can start winning financially and you can become a person who is capable of *everything*.

I will not go into detail because every step has been talked about throughout the book. This is really just a reminder to get you to focus on the right things moving forward.

Steps for Curing Financial Mediocrity

1. Decide. The first thing to do before taking any action with money is to make a damn decision. You have to *decide* that you will be wealthy and that there's nothing to stop you. Yes, you might face adversity, and you might even fail at times, but none of that will stop you. Yourself, your family, and the strangers in need of your help are all counting on you to get rich. You will not let these people down.

There's no way you're not getting rich. This is the kind of commitment you have to make before starting your journey. **If you're not certain, you'll get run over by the ones who are.** So, the first step to take on your journey toward wealth is to make a decision. Commit to getting rich *no matter what*.

"There's a redemptive power that making a choice has rather than feeling like you're an effect to all the things that are happening. Make a choice. Just decide what it's gonna be, who you're gonna be, how you're gonna do it. Just decide.

And from that point, the universe will get out of your way." -
Will Smith

2. Create income. When we've committed to getting rich, we
have to create income. I've been talking about this throughout
the entire book. Income is king.

Sell what you're good at. If you're an expert on workplace cul-
ture, go sell services as a consultant, or create a blog around it. If
you're a good receptionist, go work for a company that appreciates you and pays you well.

No matter how you decide to do it, you just have to create income. That's the first step of all wealth creation.

Can this be through a job? Absolutely. A job is actually a great
way to create your first income stream. As long as you're using
the income from your job to create additional flows of income, it's
great.

3. Increase income. The next step is to increase that first flow
of income. I'm not talking about working more hours. I'm talking
about finding a way to get paid more for your time. If it's a job,
become more valuable and do more so that your employer will
pay you more per hour. If your stream of income is a business,
find ways to improve the system, improve your product, or become better at selling your product. Whatever it takes for you to
increase and strengthen that first flow of income, do it. Income is
king.

4. Save. Don't start saving when you're making just $300 a
month. It'll take way too long to save anything significant. You
have to spend all your time and money on scaling your first income stream until it's paying you well. *Then,* you can start saving.

When your income stream is decent, that's when you should start saving. Save a large chunk of what your first income stream is providing. The more you save, the faster you'll be able to create additional flows of income and the stronger they will be. So, get your income stream to a decent height and then save as much as possible.

Don't do what most people do, though. Don't save for a rainy day. Don't save for retirement. Don't just save to save.

Why is this dumb? Because of inflation. If you let your money sit for 40, 30, or even 20 years without investing it, your money will rot. By saving for retirement, you're literally saving $100 today to eventually have what's worth $40. That's genius (nope).

Rather, you should be saving to invest. Yes, you should save a huge chunk of your income. However, you shouldn't save just to save. You should save to invest.

5. Invest. When you've saved enough money to be able to invest, it's time to acquire assets. It's time to take your hard-earned money and make it work for you. This way, your money will continue to grow by itself. Your dollars will be your little freedom fighters, your soldiers. These little soldiers will do whatever they can to grow themselves while recruiting other soldiers to do the same. Eventually, you'll have an entire army of dollars which will continuously grow on their own, without your presence. This is powerful.

I could go into all the different kinds of investing but that would require more space. My favorite kind is multi-family real estate, though.

6. Create an additional flow of income. When you're ready, and you have the time, money, energy, etc., you can create an additional flow of income. This can be a business, a book, a speaking career, consulting, etc. It can be anything that puts money in your pocket.

With these additional flows of income, you have to implement the three ingredients. Having 10 flows of income that you can't control is not ideal. This will provide stress and problems that you don't wanna have.

Having multiple flows of income that aren't scalable is discouraging and a great way to get stressed and frustrated. Limiting your income flows will put a giant limit on your wealth and opportunities.

I don't have to get into why it's not ideal to have multiple flows of income that all depend on you trading your time away. There's simply not enough time for that.

Another thing I have to mention is that your additional flows of income can be symbiotic, meaning they complement each other. This is not a must, but it's a huge advantage. With symbiotic flows of income, you can actually increase all of your flows by increasing one of them.

Let me explain.

This book is a flow of income for me. Another flow of income could be giving speeches. My speeches would contain the same type of content found in my book. This means that I can sell my speaking gigs in this book and I can sell this book at my speaking gigs. Every time I sell more books, I make more money per speech and I get more speaking opportunities. Every time I speak, I sell more books.

I can then create some kind of membership that I can sell in my book and during my speeches. I can sell my books and my speeches on this membership, too.

I can continue creating additional flows of income that all complement and strengthen each other. This is incredibly powerful.

So, having your additional flows of income be symbiotic with the others is not a must, but I would definitely recommend it. You make more money this way and it's a lot easier to handle, control, and scale.

7. Increase the additional flow. When you've created, acquired, or have purchased an additional flow of income, it's time to optimize, improve, and scale that flow. Your goal is to build it to a point where it's functioning on its own. This can be done by building systems, hiring people, or both. Eventually, this should be another money machine in your collection.

8. Repeat 4-7.

By following these steps, you can create unlimited wealth.

Now, let's get into curing personal mediocrity and becoming a person capable of huge success and achievements.

STEPS FOR CURING PERSONAL MEDIOCRITY

1. Decide. The first step of everything is to make a decision and commit to it. It's the same thing with becoming great. We have to make a decision that we will master this, this, and that. We need to decide what we want to become great at and then commit to mastering that specific skill. This can be sales, nutrition, real estate, taxes, confidence, etc.

Again, there cannot be any gray areas here. Half-assed decisions like, "I'm probably gonna practice that once in a while, if I feel like it," will not do anything good for you. Get rid of everything half-assed and gray in your life. Every decision should be black or white, 100 or zero. If you make a decision that is neither 0% or 100%, you'll end up with unsatisfying results. I mean, **I don't even know what giving 90% means. But I've heard it means *failure*.**

So, if there's a skill you could see being a valuable addition to your life, make a clear decision about how good you want to be at that. Now, saying you want to be *decent* at something is not half-assed or gray, as long as you're 100% clear on that. There's nothing wrong with not striving to become the best the world has ever seen at something. Just don't be 70% certain you want to be decent. Be 100% or 0% certain, always. Make a clear decision about which skills you'll learn and how good you'll become at each of them.

To give you some ideas, let me show you the skills, or the areas of life, I plan to master at one point. These skills, or areas of life, are all things I work on improving every single day. Some of them, I want to become pretty good at. Others, I'm trying to become the best in the world at.

Here they are in random order:

- Health
- Wealth
    - o Real Estate Investing (mostly multi-family)
- Business
    - o Entrepreneurship

     o Sales

- Peak performance

- Happiness

     o Emotions

- People

     o Psychology

Now, these things might change in the future. It's always okay to change our goals, visions, opinions, etc., as long as we're doing our best with what we know and how we think at the current moment.

2. Research and plan. The next thing to do is to find out what it takes to become great at what you want to become great at. I know exactly how I can go from where I am to being in amazing shape. I know exactly how I can go from where I am to being an incredible salesman. I know how I can go from where I am to where I want to be in every area of life. How do I know this? I researched.

So, when you've decided to become a master at finger wrestling, the next step is to research and get clear on how you're going to get there. Find places you can study, research, and find information on finger wrestling and find great ways to practice it.

How often are you gonna study? When are you gonna study? How often will you practice? When? How long should it take for you to become as good at finger wrestling as you'd like to? How much effort, time, money, energy, etc. will you put in daily?

You can definitely test out certain things before you do all this research. However, I suggest you get clear on these things before committing 100% to learning a skill. The biggest reason people quit when learning new skills is because they didn't prepare properly. They thought more of the rewards than they should've and they thought too little of the effort, time, and energy it required.

"Frustration is misplaced expectation." - Gloria Mayfield Banks

Be clear on what it's going to take for you to become as good as you want to be. I recommend underestimating the rewards and overestimating the effort. Living life this way will put you in a spot of many pleasant surprises. Don't calculate the wind to be in your back. Calculate the wind to be in your face the entire journey and then be pleasantly surprised when it isn't.

Get clear on what it's going to take. Research and plan.

3. Learn - study and practice. I wrote a lot about this in the "Master It" part in chapter 3. Studying is crucial because without it, practicing can be ineffective, difficult, and sometimes even impossible. Practicing is crucial because without it, the information you study will be *potential* power and nothing more. Potential power is useless if you don't use it. The only way to use it is to practice and implement.

4. Implement and take action. When you've learned a new skill, it's time to implement and put that skill to use. Implement what you've learned to improve your life, and others' lives, as much as possible. Use your new skill to provide value for the world. If you can't do that, then you've wasted your time and energy.

5. Repeat 1-4. Keep learning new valuable skills that can improve life for you and others. When you've implemented the skill and you've made it a part of you and your life, move on to the next valuable skill and do the same thing. Always learn, implement, and take action.

CONCLUSION

There's obviously a lot more to success, wealth, freedom, and the world-class lifestyle. However, if you keep focusing on the steps I laid out in this chapter, you will achieve extraordinary results financially and personally.

By the way, another reason I called this part "The Beginning" is because you and I are not done yet. We're only getting started. This is not the end, it's the beginning. It's the beginning of an amazing lifestyle filled with wealth, success, freedom, and joy.

However, it's also the beginning of the relationship between you and I. I hope you want more of me because I want more of you. I hope you're as excited and as obsessed as I am about reaching our potential financially, emotionally, mentally, and physically.

I have a pretty good feeling that you are fully committed to reaching your potential in all areas of life. You see, not many people look for ways to take their lives to the next level. Out of the ones who do, not many people will actually take interest in a book like this. Out of the ones who do take interest in a book like this, not many will pick it up, and even fewer will read it all the way to the end like you've done.

This should tell you something. It definitely tells me something. It tells me you're the kind of person I would love to do great things with. Again, I want to do huge things with you and I hope you're up for that, too.

At the moment, I do not have any programs, courses, memberships, etc. ready. So, for now, we'll have to keep in touch through email (Daniel@cure-mediocrity.com) and our Facebook community (www.facebook.com/groups/CureMediocrity).

Regardless of you and I staying in touch (which I'm sure we will) or not, I want to thank you for reading my book and listening to what I have to say. Keep being dedicated and committed to the world-class lifestyle, and I guarantee you'll get there. The fact that you're here right now is proof that you'll go far in life.

THANK YOU

DON'T WASTE
YOUR POTENTIAL

I hope this book made it clear that you can be great - in *all* areas of life. By gaining clarity, following proven strategies, and then taking massive, determined action toward your vision, you can do everything. You can achieve everything you've ever dreamed of and you can acquire everything you desire.

Under one condition, that is. You have to believe that it's possible. You have to be confident that you can have, do, and be everything you want to. You can do so much more than what everyone else is doing. Keep in mind, most people are living up to 2% of their potential in life. Don't be like most people. Don't let these mediocre people take you away from your dreams. Don't let them prevent you from reaching your potential and living life to the fullest.

Don't let anyone put limits on you and your capabilities. Not even yourself. You have to believe that you can have everything if you commit to having it and you take action.

You can do *anything*.

I suggest you create massive wealth, achieve freedom, travel the world, get in great shape, take care of yourself - physically and mentally, develop yourself as a person, and, most importantly, help a ton of people in the process. *Why?* Because you have the opportunities to do so. Don't waste them.

Don't waste your potential.

- Daniel Hauge

www.ingramcontent.com/pod-product-compliance
Lightning Source LLC
Chambersburg PA
CBHW051632170526
45167CB00001B/161